Copyright © 2003

All rights reserved. No part of this book may be used or reproduced in any manner whatsoever without the written permission of the Publisher. Printed in the United States of America. For information address Hyperion, 77 West 66th Street, New York, New York 10023-6298.

Library of Congress Cataloging-in-Publication Data

Pennington, Ty.

Ty's tricks / Ty Pennington—1st. ed.

p. cm.

ISBN 1-4013-0067-7

1. Dwellings—Maintenance and repair—Popular works. 2. Dwellings—Remodeling—Popular works. I. Title.

TH4817.3.P383 2003

643'.7—dc21

Design and Production by Eisenberg And Associates

First Edition

10 9 8 7 6 5 4 3 2

Hyperion books are available for special promotions and premiums. For details contact Michael Rentas, Manager, Inventory and Premium Sales, Hyperion, 77 West 66th Street, 11th floor, New York, New York 10023, or call 212-456-0133.

Cover shot by Eric Butler
All interiors photographed by Erica Georges Dines

Contributing Photographers
Joe Schmelzer
Jonathan Jumonville
Jeff Schirmer
Ty Pennington

TY'S tricks

by Ty Pennington

HYPERION NEW YORK

The realization of writing a "do-it-yourself" book, then trying to "do-it-yourself" was an eye-opening experience. I would like to thank everyone who helped make "doing-it" possible.

First and foremost I want to thank my "Precious," Drea; without her persistence, patience, and sense of humor this would have never been finished and probably never started. They broke the mold after they made you. Truly an Original!

I would like to thank everyone, especially Gretchen Young at Hyperion, for their incredible help and dedication to making this happen. Everyone at Eisenberg and Associates for their creativity, patience and great work ethic, you guys are the shiznit. Michael Broussard the "book dealer," Susan Haber, Jody Simon, and Andrea "Drea" Bock, my management team — you guys ROCK! The cast and crew and everyone involved with making *Trading Spaces* such a fantastic fun show to be on. Especially my favorite E.P.'s, "Executive Producers" Denise Cramsey and Leigh Seamen, who are not afraid to take a "Risk." A personal shout out to my family and friends whom I merely imitate, I owe it all to you.

CONTENTS

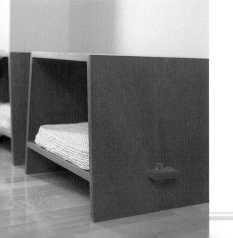

Ty's Tricks

Before there is any confusion regarding the contents of this book, this is not a "magic" book. This book will not teach you how to make a rabbit or an airplane disappear into a hat or the dry thin air of the Las Vegas desert. I am not David Copperfield. I cannot teach you the the hat, and my luggage never showed up in baggage claim. I am, however, an artist, designer, and fairly decent carpenter. I have an eye for detail, an ear for demands, a quick-witted mind, and experienced hands, and I've felt the joy and pain, not to mention the strain, of creatively solving design, renovation, and home-repair problems by being extremely resourceful. I am not, however, an expert in every facet of home repair. I know a lot about some things and enough about others to know when to hire professional help. I have renovated a warehouse, my own house, and countless homes across America as the carpenter on the TV show *Trading Spaces* on The Learning Channel. I have written this book to share the laughs, lessons, and love as well as the pride and confidence you gain by doing it yourself. When you open this book, I hope it will help you open your mind, your heart, and your eyes to see the endless possibilities, new ideas, and capabilities you have inside yourself, your home, and your hands to accomplish almost anything by doing it yourself. All you need is a little know-how, a little time, a little help, and a few tools. By using this book as a fun guide or really functional tool you might even give yourself a makeover without all the feng shui.

This book could have been called "More for Less — Cheap and Easy Tricks to Do It Yourself with Style" because, more or less, it is a how-you-can-do-it book for doing more while spending less and creating style instead of stress. It is meant to be easy, fun, and informal as well as enlightening, inspiring, and informative. It is not a typical home-improvement book. This book, like its author, takes a unique and sometimes comedic approach to prepare you for the twists and turns, re-dos and re-turns, miscommunications and frequent frustrations that inevitably come with any home renovation. It is informal but informative. It's a hands-on how-to book to keep your home-repair projects from getting out of hand. This book is designed to be a guide for anyone willing to start the job and finish the journey, down the unmarked and unpredictable path of do-it-yourself home improvement by blazing his or her own trail with more style and efficiency while spending less time, money, and energy. It gives step-by-step advice and instructions to help avoid the hazards and havoc that repairs and remodeling can wreak upon an unsuspecting home! It's a home-work handbook for the "screw-it and do-it-yourselfers." It's a tool for using tools. It's a measurement of rules, it gives direction for finding a direction in which you will have to choose. It's a map book, notebook, repair book, and quote book; it's a scrap book, fact book, tool book, and hopefully a cool book. But in the end, it's just a book written to help you realize that if you visualize and improvise, you can build anything you dream.

introduction

Even if you've always thought that a Phillips head was a flathead and an eight-penny nail sounds way too expensive, it's okay. Phillip's head is flat, but that's his problem, and eight cents a nail is outrageous. I'm kidding, but the truth is that anyone, even you, can save money by doing some of your own home renovation and repair, no matter how inexperienced you are, no matter how lousy you are with your hands, no matter how much you think you can't do it. It's okay. I'll bet you're great at pinching pennies. That's good because I can help with the rest.

By the time you get to the last page of this book, I hope you will have laughed, learned, and left with newfound confidence. I'm sure that you'll be ready to try new ideas, trust your instincts, and, in the end, be thrilled at the thought of saving enough ducats for a trip to Hawaii. There you'll be, relaxing under the shade of a coconut palm tree, swaying in the breeze of gentle winds, sipping on a Mai Tai with a little umbrella in the glass. You'll meet interesting people from faraway places and eventually you will overhear someone talking about the nightmares of remodeling, projects started and never finished, houses that swallow up entire college funds, and so-called contractors who are more into the CON than keeping up their end of the CONTRACT.

Meanwhile, you'll be sporting a smug little smirk, not saying a word, just nodding as if to say, "I can only imagine." Then you'll pause and ask your honey to pass the sunscreen. A distant radio will be playing Frank Sinatra's "I Did It My Way" and you'll feel fantastic knowing you will never again be the one getting burned!

Now before we get started, I'll begin by telling you that because I supposedly know it all, many of you think that I was granted divine wisdom and blessed with billions of years of experience in construction. You may have imagined me teaching the ancient Egyptians stone carving, or sharing my plumbing and irrigation tips with the Romans, or you might picture me giving seminars on working with dovetail joints and jigs in order for the Vikings to build bigger boats for their pillaging gigs. Now seems like a good time to remind you that I AM ONLY HUMAN, I DON'T KNOW EVERYTHING. I MAKE A LOT OF MISTAKES AND SOMETIMES SMELL BAD, BUT I'M CREATIVE AND PERSISTENT. AND I WILL FINISH THE PROJECT.

Well, enough about me already, let's talk about me. Let's see, from an early age I have been drawing and building things. Demolition seemed to be one of my earliest vocations.

I've always enjoyed working with my hands. In fact, one of my earliest memories is of preparing a surprise Sunday breakfast for my mother. Along with my older brother, Wynn, as my frontline prep cook, we prepared a feast. Eighteen strips of bacon, a full dozen eggs, and a container of premade pancake batter we found in the fridge. It was such a thrill to see the "surprised" look on our mom's face. First we gave her a wakeup call by banging pots and pans together over her head as she lay asleep. Next, we noticed even more surprise as we proudly displayed our "breakfast of champions" that was elegantly spread all over the kitchen. Our smiles of pride gave way to shrieks of fear as my mother's biggest surprise was finding her brand-new couch covered with bacon grease, pancake batter, and a dozen raw eggs. Tears of joy weren't the only things running that early Sunday morning. In fact, I learned I was pretty quick on my feet and that I had lightning-quick reflexes. I also had my first lesson in constructive criticism. Needless to say, I gave up a career in the culinary arts and focused on more viable occupations, such as remodeling and redesigning pre-existing furniture.

I started redesigning the furniture in our house, *all* the furniture in our house, including a piano. I would work and work, trying new things until I would eventually grow tired, but not nearly as tired as my mother was of my constant redecorating. I was never satisfied with leaving anything the way I found it. Traditional thinking just didn't work for me. As a child psychologist, my mother recognized the artistic and creative spirit in me and seemed to really understand that I needed ways to express myself. So she told me, "It's time that you build a place of your own. With your own style, your own furniture." She packed me a knapsack, a thermos full of soup, a hammer, and a box of nails and said, "Now I know you're scared but you've done such great work here with my place, I know your new place will be even better. But listen carefully because this is important: You will not be allowed back in this house until you have gotten all of your designing, decorating, and building urges out of your system, and you will do no more to this house, 'cause it's just a little overdone. Do you understand?"

That day I realized she was right; I needed to build a place where I could say, Yes, I built this. This is me, this is mine, and I made this with my bare hands.

I begged my brother to help me, but he only smiled and said no. I offered up a few collectible comics in my collection worth a few trips to Dairy Queen and pretty soon the neighborhood got wind of the Comic Collectors' Construction Sale. Two comics for one hour of work. Pretty soon I had a full crew with a lead foreman and, of course, me as project manager/designer. Some kids brought tools from their dads' garages, and by dusk we, I mean *I*, had built a three-story tree house between three tall trees, thirty-five feet high, with an observation deck, main living area, a galley for storage, and a rope ladder. It was beautiful. Decked in rough cut pine, framed in 2x6 and railed with cottonwood and ash. What a wonderful feeling that was. The sun going down, all of us still sweating, the sound of saws tearing through green and dry wood, the sap and dust, the blisters on our hands, the dirt on our faces. We didn't have a single argument that day; instead, everyone focused on the job at hand. Staying true to my design, of course swaying from my vision occasionally if materials and tools were not available. But ultimately we were, I mean *I* was, completely satisfied with the job well done.

That evening, with the sun at my back, standing on the eighth wonder of the world, I felt it was my own personal Taj Mahal. From the top deck I looked down at my mother's house and saw her looking out the kitchen window. She smiled and began applauding, as if to say, "I knew you could do it, and thank God you did it outside of the house." I knew then that I could do anything I put my mind to. No matter the cost or the time, I would find a way. This was only the beginning . . .

I didn't let on then, but I had learned a great deal that day. I learned about myself and what I could accomplish, and I learned even more about working with other people, how different opinions, different ideas, different tools, made a difference.

But mainly I realized what a wonderful motivator my mother was. Without her, none of this would have happened and it might have taken me years to recognize my true calling. She is an amazing person, gifted with the ability to find people's strengths and help them overcome their flaws while building their confidence.

Building that tree house is where I discovered my passion for home repair and remodeling. Throughout most of my years I have worked off and on in some form of home remodeling, from framing to finishing to furniture. Over the years I've done a little bit of everything. Eventually I went into business for myself, renovating homes for clients. With three partners, I converted an 18,000-square-foot warehouse space into seven functioning apartments. From the drywall to the drains to the dimmer switches, it definitely pays to do it yourself. But it pays even more when you sell the real estate. So after selling the warehouse and getting my one-quarter share, I had just enough funds to finance a fixer-upper. Finally a house of my own, or a shack, really. Well, let's call it a Victorian bungalow.

Meanwhile, along with renovating homes for clients as well as working on my own home, I moonlighted as an actor/model, auditioning for all kinds of commercials. It's probably no coincidence that most of the commercials I landed promoted products used to ease aching muscles or treat rashes caused by over-sweating. Then one day I got a call from my commercial agent asking, "Dude, you're pretty handy with a hammer, right? There's this home improvement show that is looking for a sarcastic carpenter and we thought of you."

I hope at least some of you know me as the carpenter on *Trading Spaces,* where along with providing a little comic relief, I have been designing and building furniture, and creating solutions to design problems with unique approaches for utilizing space, materials, and time. All the while revamping a room, well actually two, with a budget of only $1,000 in each room. My favorite part of the job is showing homeowners how to close their eyes and open their minds to new ideas and new techniques that, if not always chic, are definitely unique. I have such a great time watching the homeowners laugh and learn at the same time, teaching without preaching from my experience in home improvement. Sharing how-to advice for spending half the time and half the price. It gives me great satisfaction helping the homeowners realize that they can do it themselves with a little help, a little know-how, and the right tools. With two full days of backbreaking labor, anything can be accomplished! After it all, finally seeing the fruits of their labor revealed to their friends and neighbors, some scream and cheer while others cry streams of tears, and we all are reminded that beauty is truly in the eye of the beholder.

But whether they loved it or loathed it, most of them said: "I would definitely do it again." "I had so much fun working with my hands and learning new ideas." "Ty's little tips were so helpful and, oh yeah, I'm definitely gonna keep working with power tools." "I just can't believe we did it all in two days. We painted the walls and the ceilings, installed all new flooring, and helped Ty build all new furniture that totally rocks!! But man, I am tired."

I've got the best job in the world. I get to create new projects and work with great people every day. Seeing how happy the experience makes the homeowners, giving them newfound confidence to take on the everyday obstacles that life throws their way. I wanted to share that joy with everyone not able to "trade spaces" on the show. And since the show involves me as the cast invading homes of others, I thought it would be cool to have you invade mine.

a.

b.

c.

The living room is full of artful creations all painted, designed, and built or found. (pictured) *a.* The indoor tree is a crape myrtle found in a rubbish pile, then set in a peach crate filled with cement. *b.* The orb lights were made from found objects and placed on stands used from old fondue kits. *c.* The *Fowl* painting done by Ty is mounted in a frame made with tongue-and-groove flooring, Plexiglas, and shims.

Each room in the house was painted a different color. By using consecutive colors on the color wheel, they create a natural flow from avocado (green-yellow) to mustard (yellow) to cantaloupe (yellow-orange). See Choosing Colors.

The bedroom was completely renovated from floor to ceiling
using recycled or reinvented materials. *(pictured)* The
picture windows were salvaged and the Shoji screens were
made with leftover Plexi and tongue-and-groove cypress.
I converted mud trays into stainless steel plant holders.
The sundial wall art and floor-standing candleholders were
made from old piano parts.

chapter 1

HOW I BUILT A CHAMPAGNE HOUSE ON A BEER BUDGET

As a carpenter on the television show *Trading Spaces*, I engage in what is more like "invading places." Accompanied by crazed designers, I barge in on willing but apprehensive homeowners, disturbing their nests and sometimes leaving them in tears from either exhaustion or fear. So, I thought that it would be cool to "trade spaces" with you. I'm inviting you into my house for a change.

Letting you see firsthand, what I've built by hand, how you save when you can, do-it-yourself with a plan, while living large in Ty-land.

But before I take you through my house, let me explain how and why I bought one in the first place! Along with my brother and two other partners, I had recently renovated an old two-story warehouse, converting it into seven loft apartments; I finished out one of these apartments for myself and it turned out pretty swank.

Although we didn't make much money converting that "diamond in the rough," we did get a good return on what we had invested, which was our time. Anyway, living in the converted warehouse was great because I had a shop downstairs where I could build cool furniture, sometimes using some of the old parts from pianos left over from the building's warehouse days (see Chapter 2, Cool Stuff: Building Outside the Box). Now, if I describe the downstairs as cool, I would definitely have to say that the upstairs was hot. Especially when it's August in Atlanta and you're living in a loft with windows that won't open. Oh, and did I mention that we had no central heating or air conditioning? So, when the building sold, I was ready to step into the ring-o-fire of relocating and renovating a house of my own.

I bought my house exactly one year before being hired as a carpenter on *Trading Spaces*.

The house was an old Victorian bungalow located near the oldest park in Atlanta. It was being sold as a bank foreclosure and was selling super-cheap. I knew that if I didn't jump on it, the house, along with my money, would be gone in a week. I had exactly $15,000 left from selling the warehouse. I made a down payment of $5,000, which left me with $10,000 to start the renovation.

Now, $10,000 may sound like a lot of money, but when it comes to remodeling a house, it's barely enough to scratch the surface. We're talking serious shoestring budget.

The moment I walked through the door of the house that was to become my home, I knew I was going to have to get creative. With a little TLC and a lot of OT, I knew I could turn that turn-of-the-century eyesore into a modern-day miracle.

The house was all original except for an addition to the rear of the house, built sometime in the seventies. The original frame was built in "shotgun" style, with two rooms and a very small kitchen/bath on each side. The seventies-something renovations converted the house into a three-bedroom, two-bath home, making it larger than the other shotgun bungalows built throughout this historic neighborhood.

Except for termite damage, structural damage, corroded pipes, uneven flooring, and useless windows and doors, the house was in pretty good shape. Well, let's just say that it had plenty of character. Another diamond in the rough!

The good news was that the walls were in pretty good shape because new drywall had been installed over the plaster. Also, new electrical wiring had been run throughout the house. Most of the real work to be done was cosmetic. Now for the bad news. The kitchen was a wreck, sporting a hideous purple countertop. Then there was the peeling linoleum floor that left off where a new floor began. This marked the start of the old renovation, which featured lovely half-walls installed to separate the room and make it smaller. There was also a sliding glass door, streaked from old age, which, if it wasn't stuck, would lead into the backyard. Oh, and did I mention the drop ceiling filled with asbestos ceiling tiles? I won't even tell you about the smell, but I think you get the idea. And that was just the kitchen!

I figured that my first priority was to eat in a clean kitchen, so I decided to start there. I had worked with my friend Will installing cement board and laying tile for other clients. The one thing I knew for sure about laying tile is that the materials are fricking seriously heavy. Tiles come in boxes weighing up to thirty-five pounds. You can bet that anything called cement board isn't going to be light. Throw in a few twenty-five-pound bags of mortar and grout, and you've thrown your back out before you even lay your first tile. So Will wasn't surprised when I decided to quit working on my house for a while. However, he was surprised when I called him again later to ask to borrow his double-suspension "man-van." I needed his vehicle in order to carry all the

The totem shelf is a simple, natural design consisting of wooden shelves that slide into grooves; since they are not glued or nailed, they can be moved and arranged differently.

tiles I would need for my new kitchen floor in one trip. I, of course, had to agree to help paint his house in exchange for the use of the van.

I decided to use Spanish terra-cotta or Mexican tiles not only because they matched the color of my tongue-and-groove flooring but also because they are easy to install, extremely durable, and hide imperfections in both the subflooring and the installation (see Tile with a Smile, page 147).

Now that I had gotten the tile home, I needed to raise half of the kitchen floor 6 inches before I could start on the tile. By using plywood, I finally got the floors fairly even. Then I used latex thin set to level the seam and screwed down cement board.

Cool Fact: Mexican or Spanish tiles have little foot or paw prints indented in the tiles as a result of children and dogs running along the Mexican beaches and then running across the tiles where they are left to dry. Seems like just the right material for a kitchen, considering the traffic an average kitchen gets.

Of course, after raising the floor, I would have to raise the sliding glass door, which meant installing a new header.

Anyway, after pulling off the baseboards and masking off the ones I couldn't pull off, I mixed the mortar and set the tiles, soaked my back and knees for the night, and then grouted and cleaned the following day.

Using Mexican tiles made the job cheap (about $2 a tile) and easy (tile is masking free). And the tile made the room look totally huge when it totally wasn't. Doing the job myself was not only good for my ego but also was financially rewarding as well. The materials cost around $1,500, but my labor was free!

Doing it yourself is, without a doubt, a way to save money. When you have a *really* tight budget, you can save additional dollars by using functional but unconventional materials. This allows you to save on costs without losing style (see Chapter 2, Cool Stuff: Building Outside the Box).

For example, placing tile in the kitchen ensured not only a clean but also a durable surface to walk on. I decided to give the countertops a workable surface as well. Instead of replacing the purple countertop with the typical countertop materials, laminate and particleboard, I used a butcher-block alternative: thick, durable, prelaminated hardwood and American oak. I also mixed my favorite Malaysian redwoods with the oak, all for under $3 a square foot!

All woodwork needs a sealer, and polyurethane makes a great one. It is waterproof and easy to clean. Another good choice is mineral oil, which should be used if you plan to do any cutting, slicing, or chopping on the wooden surface. *The good news is that mineral oil is also a laxative!*

After I finished the countertop and built a little "nook" supported by galvanized pipe and floor flange (also very cheap materials), my cooking area was almost done. All I needed now was a kitchen sink. I replaced the old stainless steel sink with a heavier, stronger white porcelain sink that I bought at a salvage yard for $35. Then I hooked up the water lines, fixed all the leaks, and sealed the edges with silicone caulk (see Chapter 7, Flooring). I ended up spending around $120 for my new countertops and sink. That is Pinching Pennies, People! And it looked killer.

Now, seeing as how the new theme of the kitchen was turning out to be all earth tones, featuring the beautiful natural wood countertops and the terracotta flooring, I thought that I would continue the earthy color scheme right up to the ceiling. First, I had to rip down the existing drop ceiling and tiles. Then, I created a new ceiling and substrate with two-by-fours and 3/4-inch plywood, cutting holes for some totally cool can lights to be installed. Then I nailed prefinished Brazilian cherry flooring to the ceiling (see Chapter 7, Flooring), using a finish nailer. I relied on an electrician friend to hook up the can lighting. He gave me a deal, charging me only by the hour, and I'm here to tell you that a few hours of professional electrical help are well worth the cost, because you don't want to be on the wrong end of a hot wire. Trust me there, Sparky.

I have to say, I think the kitchen turned out great especially when compared to what it looked like before I started. In fact, the change was as dramatic as any of the changes that you see in our before-and-after shots on *Trading Spaces*.

The kitchen needed a lot of work. The floors were two separate levels covered in old linoleum floor tiles. The half walls only made the room look half the size. And the dingy drop ceiling had to be dropped. I gutted and replaced everything, I mean everything, including the kitchen sink.

AFTER

The kitchen is the room where everyone
hangs out, so I wanted to make it fun.
Since it also faces south, it is the brightest
room to work in. I've always loved art classes
and mixing work with play. So I used
bright, primary colors to inspire creativity
and add elements of learning in the room.

9

So HOW MUCH DID IT COST
To COMPLETE MY KITCHEN?
SLIDING GLASS DOOR $400
MEXICAN TILE FLOOR $1,500
COUNTER TOPS & SINK $120
TONGUE & GROOVE $1,000
CEILING
CAN LIGHTS $350
PLUNGER LIGHTS $6
CLIPBOARDS $4

TOTAL $3,380

I could have saved more by using maple plywood instead of Brazilian cherry on the ceiling, but sometimes you have to spend a little more in order to get more when you sell your house. And that, my friend, is all about the look.

So the kitchen was almost finished, except for a few last things. I needed a few hanging lights over the kitchen nook. To put a little light, not to mention a little humor, on the subject, I made hanging lights out of ordinary (but stylish) household plungers (see Chapter 2, Cool Stuff: Building Outside the Box). They ended up looking pretty cool, a bit like Japanese lanterns, adding to the minimal, Zenlike designs that flow through the interior, exterior, and furniture of my house. I also needed a little more color in the kitchen than just the "cantaloupe" chair rail and that flat white paint. So, in order to save money, space, and, most important, messages, I installed red, orange, yellow, and black construction paper on chrome clipboards and mounted them to the wall. These primary and secondary colors (see Choosing Colors, page 123) complemented the cantaloupe chair rail as well as pulling the room together by tying the chrome into the hardware and appliances. The clipboard arrangement gave me simple, clean, industrial art that was not only beautiful in form but

To make the kitchen a durable place to work, entertain, and feed the mind full of bright ideas, I used ceramic tiles on the floors, and hardwood flooring on the countertops and ceiling. I created "think pads" using bright-colored construction paper on chrome clipboards. Those match the stainless steel stove, new kitchen hardware, and red school chairs that were found in a salvage yard. For fun, I turned household plungers into hanging lights. Everything in the room was built or found for almost nothing or made cheap, quick, and easy.

quite functional as well. It gave the room a bold splash of color that would change with every new color of paper left in place on the clipboard. I then added a long black and white "action" painting (from my kung fu series) to the opposite wall. It not only complemented the clipboard colors (especially the black) but was also a nice contrast as well. Now my kitchen was complete.

The next most important room to me in the house was the bathroom. Not only is it important to the resale value of the house, but it is also important in the event of an overactive bladder. If you have ever lived with another human, then you know the joy of living in a house with more than one bathroom. Luckily, my house had two, so when my guest was "going to the party," I could too.

The guest bathroom was small but complete, with a tub, shower, toilet, and sink that looked like it had been custom fit for a small child. The sink was wall mounted and so low that it literally hit you above the knees. I thought it was kind of cool, so I left it intact. I did, however, change a few other things. I wanted my guests to feel that taking a bath should be like going on a relaxing journey to a tropical island. *So I said to myself "Phuket" (pronounced* Pû-ket)*, which is an island off the coast of Thailand.* With that theme in mind, I grabbed the table saw, ripped some bamboo poles in half (see Chapter 2, Cool Stuff: Building Outside the Box), and nailed them to one wall with a finish nailer. They extended up from the floor to the ceiling and gave you the feeling that you were peeking inside a bamboo forest (*off the coast of Ty-land*). I replaced an old glass fixture with a wastebasket made from burlap encased in resin that I bought at a thrift store for $2. I covered the ugly linoleum floors with leftover tongue-and-groove flooring from the master bedroom. I "fluffed" the room with accessories ranging from tiki god candles to stalks of lemongrass (which is used as a spice in the other Thailand). But my absolute favorite bathroom fixture was the toilet-paper holder. I made it by screwing a curtain rod holder to the wall and sliding a piece of bamboo over it (see Chapter 2, Cool Stuff: Building Outside the Box).

I lit the guest bathroom using a low-watt bulb and a wastebasket, then used bamboo for a wall treatment as well as a toilet- paper holder.

To keep my own personal style of feng-shui flowing, I created a "Buddha-Fall" koi pond and Zen garden by using discarded slate roof shingles, planting bamboo, and building a deck with Asian-style planters.

In keeping with the harmony of the house, I transplanted several varieties of bamboo to create a zen garden complete with a "Buddha"ful waterfall and koi pond. Then I built a deck and stylish Asian planters out of pressure treated lumber. I used unwanted but not unusable slate roof shingles that had been thrown out in Vern's neighborhood, nailing them to a concrete retaining wall that I had poured after digging out the pond in, yes, two days (see Cool Stuff: Building Outside the Box).

After a long vacation from renovation, whether it be peeing or bathing in a bamboo forest, or meditating and fishing for koi in a zen garden, it's always nice to come home to a comfortable, clean, and private bedroom with a bath.

But if you thought the kitchen needed work, you should have seen the bedroom. The floors, or lack thereof, were covered with what used to be a light blue, wall-to-wall seventies shag carpet that smelled like a kennel, even after it had been cleaned! The room did, however, have one thing that is quite useful in a master bedroom: a walk-in closet. It also had a bay window overlooking the backyard. And most important, it had a master bathroom complete with not only an interesting puke-yellow-green toilet but also an awesome bedpan-shaped shower to match. The shower was so swank, and so "seventies," that I almost installed a disco ball in the bedroom, but I couldn't take the excessive "funk." So the first thing that I did in the bedroom was *"cut a rug"* and rip out the carpet and *"the funk."*

Before I laid the hardwood floors, I wanted to add both space and light by installing two huge windows. This meant that I had to install another long header to span the length of both windows. But that part of the job, ripping off the siding, cutting out the drywall and such, would be easy. Reframing the wall without disturbing the electrical outlets, not to mention lifting two huge 5-foot windows into place, would not be easy. Once the windows were in, I replaced the drywall (see Chapter 5, Walls), then finished the window with a window seat made from the "truck-flooring" in the kitchen. I used Douglas fir to build the frame and leftover tongue-and-groove cypress for the trim. I left

the tongue, but more important, the groove, on the lumber for a pretty cool reason. I created "shoji" screens by sliding 1/4-inch white Plexiglas into the groove to help hold the acrylic in place (see Chapter 2, Cool Stuff: Building Outside the Box). This was not only nice to look at, but served a function as well. It allowed the Plexiglas to act as another pane, thereby insulating any large window from hot and cold air. Also, it worked as a light-diffusing screen, casting shadows but not graphic images of what goes on in your bedroom to your viewing audience of neighbors. I covered the kitchen windows with the same material but used "backward installed hinges" to grip them in place. *Now the reason I covered those windows was because I wasn't enjoying "the neighbor's show."*

After I finished the "bedroom with a view" windows, I repaired the drywall by mudding and sponging the joints (see Chapter 5, Walls). Finally, I was ready to recover the floors.

The bedroom was the only room in the house that wasn't covered with old tongue and groove, so the carpet had been nailed straight to the joists. It had been an addition, and the only flooring installed was a plywood subfloor covered with the funky shag carpet.

The good news was that the bedroom subfloor was fairly level; the bad news was that flooring isn't cheap. I found some prefinished oak flooring that cost $3 a square foot through an ad in the paper. Trust me, it's worth paying fifty cents more a foot to buy it finished. So I rented a floor nailer and had the job done in two days. Good times on kneepads (see Chapter 7, Flooring)! The trick to getting a great-looking floor is to remove all the base molding, then leave a 1/2-inch gap between the new flooring and the wall, for expanding and contracting caused by humidity. (This is especially true if you live in the humid South.) I covered about 700 square feet of floor and the job cost around $2,100 in materials.

There was still one room left before I could claim that I was finished with my bedroom. That was my bathroom, *the* most interesting bathroom I've ever seen. I thought it deserved something a little special. I built a vanity using the same truck flooring as I did in the kitchen. Then I "mixed" things by using a chrome salad bowl for a sink! (See Chapter 2, Cool Stuff: Building Outside the Box.)

I used a hole saw, and a little plumber's putty, and twisted down the flange. Then I reattached the water lines (see Chapter 8, Plumbing) to a brand new faucet. Toss in some Teflon tape, a toothbrush, and some sweat from a plumber's back, and you have got yourself a little sink-it-yourself salad.

To tile the bathroom, I used a latex leveler and then screwed down cement board on top of it. But in order to tile the floor, I had to remove the toilet. I tiled underneath it and then raised the flange by adding a second one. (See Chapter 8, Plumbing.) By doing this, I made sure the seal between the new tile floor and the toilet was tight, preventing a possible future flood from a flush. I used white ceramic 1-inch tile that comes enmeshed together in square 1-foot sections. After the tile was set, I finished grouting and sealed the cracks with a grout sealer that can be bought at any tile store. It keeps the tile from getting dirty with mildew stains that are easily visible on a white floor. I could have used more contemporary materials for the floor, anything from pebble stones or slate to broken tiles creating a mosaic. But I figured that with a salad bowl for a sink, not to mention a puke-green shower shaped like a bedpan, it was enough "originality" for one bathroom. Besides, trying to find a color that goes well with puke-green is not that easy in the end. I thought it was best to leave it with a clean look, not only for me but in the event that the house was sold to someone not exactly keen on getting clean inside a bedpan. The tiles weren't cheap, but it was a small space and as usual, my labor was free. I spent $85 on truck flooring to build the vanity and only $3 on the salad bowl sink. So, altogether, the bathroom materials cost a total of $293. Not bad.

Now, even though the master bathroom was finished, no master bedroom is complete without a bed fit for a king. If there is one thing I have realized in the hard days and nights of working overtime to beat the clock (Think: *Trading Spaces*) or save a buck (Think: doing it yourself), sleeping in a comfortable bed is the most "quality time" your back and booty ever get. So I wanted to put a little quality time into building a really beautiful bed and other furniture to match.

It was a challenge to create a bedroom as unique as the shower enclosure in the master bath, especially when it looks like a hospital bedpan. To match the stylish shower, I used a salad bowl for a sink.

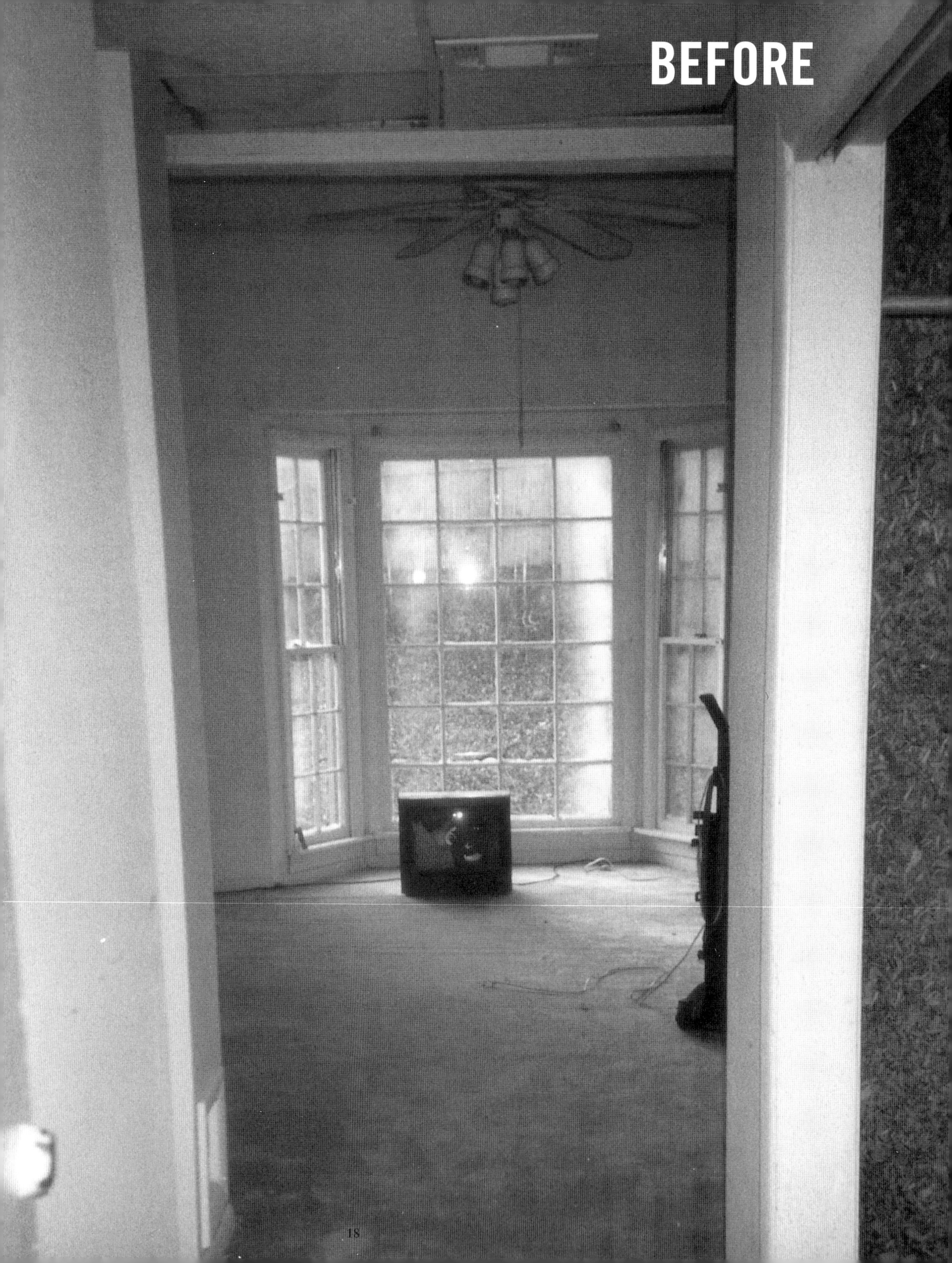

AFTER

This room was quite a makeover. I replaced the funky carpet and ceiling tiles with tongue-and-groove flooring, as well as installing new windows and creating furniture and a variety of accessories.

A QUALI-TY PRODUCT

I had bought a hand-me-down king-size bed from my brother a few months before, and I am sure some of you will agree that *once you go king-size, you never go back*. So the bed would need to be big, but it didn't have to be bulky. In order to save space, I designed it to be low to the ground, with cantilevered sidetables attached to the frame. I found dark orange Brazilian cherry that had been damaged and discounted at a local lumber yard (as seen on a *Trading Spaces* Chicago episode). Then I designed and built it to look like a platform bed.

So by skirting the edges with 6-inch-wide boards resting on 8-inch runners, and hiding the box spring, it gave the illusion of being a continuous platform without wasting money and time on extra wood. This gave me enough wood to build a "saddle bench" and matching ottomans. These were glued and held together by square pegs in square mortised holes without using one screw or nail. I sealed the wood on both the bed and benches with tung oil, leaving a beautiful natural finish. I centered the bed underneath the giant window, using it as a headboard. After I placed cushions on the bench and ottomans, the room was almost finished except for a few minor accessories. The bedside tables needed lamps so I wouldn't have to get out of bed to turn the lights

(pictured) The stylish shower enclosure is puke-green and shaped like a bedpan. It is one of the few things I did not replace in the house. The sundial clock and candle holders are made from old piano parts. The incense burner and lights are accessories designed and built for my company FU (Furniture Unlimited) and sold online at my website, tythehandyguy.com

The master bedroom needed a few bedside table lamps. So I created tai-lights out of Chinese placemats, fiberglass, sheeting, and a good piece of ash.

The saddle ottomans and bench have a minimalist design, held together with only wooden pegs and glue. For extra comfort, pillows can be placed on top or simply stored below.

down, especially when getting out of bed in the "heat of the moment" could create an awkward, even more "heated" moment. Using some old ash wood I had stacked in the woodpile, I made matching bedside lights that could be either desktop or wall mounted. After running the 1-foot-square pieces through the table saw to make three parallel grooves on each side of the board, I cupped fiberglass sheeting and a Chinese placemat around a two-bulb light fixture to create "tai-lights." I brought in a sundial clock and two 5-foot-tall "King Snake" candleholders I had already made out of old piano parts. So after the final touches, I was left to my master bedroom, which was well built and well lit, all on the investment of my lower back, which was pretty well spent.

It really is amazing what can be accomplished by doing it yourself. You are learning by doing and earning while learning. You save your money but spend your time. But as your home evolves, so does your mind. With every new problem that your house throws at you, from shrinking in size as your family multiplies to expanding between gaps and causing squeaks and ugly cracks, you'll be ready for every challenge, and remember when you were home-work challenged.

Making ends meet is challenging enough. Making a deadline on a shoestring budget is straight up hard. Let's see if I was able to take the challenge of remodeling a house floor to ceiling with only $10,000. Here is the itemized list of the materials plus the cost of hired help (see Hiring a Handyperson, page 67).

RFN# 0509-2288-954-0303-3110

KITCHEN
TILES/MORTAR/GROUT   1500.00
COUNTERTOP/SINK   130.00
SLIDING GLASS DOOR   400.00
TONGUE-AND-GROOVE CEILING/ELECTRICAL   130.00
PLUNGER LIGHTS   8.00

SUBTOTAL   3386.00

PHUKET BATHROOM
TONGUE-AND-GROOVE FLOORING   120.00
WASTEBASKET LIGHT FIXTURE   2.00
BAMBOO FOREST   0.00

SUBTOTAL   122.00

MASTER BEDROOM
SALVAGED WINDOWS   400.00
SHOJI SCREEN   150.00
HEADER/FRAME   100.00
CHERRY TONGUE-AND-GROOVE CEILING   1000.00
OAK FLOORING

MASTER BATHROOM
TILE/MORTAR/GROUT   200.00
VANITY LUMBER   85.00
SALAD BOWL SINK   3.00
SUBTOTAL   5033.00

ZEN GARDEN/KOI POND
CEMENT BAGS   60.00
RUBBER LINE/PUMP   210.00
COPPER FLASHING   90.00
DECK/LUMBER   1000.00

SUBTOTAL   1360.00

TOTAL   10003.00

STORE #5092
SEQ # 509221231

Instead of throwing this old paint can in the garbage, I reused it as an outdoor lantern by drilling holes and placing a candle in it.

"One man's trash is another man's treasure."

2

chapter

COOL STUFF

BUILDING OUTSIDE THE BOX

One of the biggest challenges I have faced as a carpenter on *Trading Spaces* (besides dealing with the demented demanding designers) is trying to rebuild a room on basically a flat-broke budget, which isn't easy. In the slogans for the Boy Scouts and the army, they say "Be prepared" and "Be all you can be." My slogan is "Be resourceful" and of course "Be very afraid," as well as "B-12," which is more of a childish look on life, but that's another story.

There is also the saying "You can get something for nothing." I don't believe that's true. I believe "You can make something for nothing." It all depends on how resourceful you are willing to be. The old saying "One man's trash is another man's treasure" couldn't be any closer to the truth. For example, South Africa is a third-world country lacking food, wealth, and even electricity in most of its remote uncivilized land. Yet, every day, modern man tries to run telephone wire across its great sprawling land. Every night the local tribes of men and women climb the telephone poles and remove the wire and weave it into hats, baskets, and jewelry, which they sell along with toys made out of Coca-Cola and Pepsi-Cola cans to the tourists. Now, you see, *that* is being resourceful. Those South Africans find materials made for one purpose and use them for another. Of course, they stole the telephone wire, but they didn't need "call waiting," they needed cash for food. (Besides, they receive messages the old-fashioned way, by running eighty-five miles and delivering by hand.)

To take on the challenge of making something for nothing, you must be very resourceful and do it yourself by hand. It can be a bit of a struggle, but it's so rewarding and fun to see what you can create by using unconventional materials — meaning those materials that you purchase for very little money or find for almost nothing — to build something that's both beautiful and functional.

To renovate my "historic" home, I had to be very resourceful. I used several unconventional materials to serve in a variety of really cool functions. I used plungers to make hanging lights in the kitchen, a wastebasket for a fixture in the bathroom, and a salad bowl for a sink. In this chapter, I will show you how to turn old slate roof shingles into a beautiful koi pond and waterfall (Buddha-fall). And I'll show you ways to use tongue-and-groove flooring to create cool countertops, beautiful ceilings, and sharp shoji screens that slide into the groove and give you insulated privacy when you are nude. Here are some of the unconventional materials I used for building outside the box. Be on the lookout for my special toilet-paper holder, which truly rocks.

This sundial clock was made out of old piano keys, cut with a miter saw then notched and glued to a knitting ring.

plunger lights

TOOLS YOU WILL NEED	MATERIALS YOU WILL NEED
Drill with 3/8-inch drill bit	Plunger(s) Light fixture kit 3/8-inch washer and nut Tubular 40-watt bulb

1. To make a hanging light out of a plunger, the first thing you have to do is find a plunger that is light enough in color to allow the light to shine through it. (Try hardware stores, Home Depot, or Kmart). Try to find one that is shaped like a "ribbed" Japanese lantern.

2. Unscrew the handle portion of the plunger. Then use a 3/8-inch drill bit and drill through the plastic top of the plunger head, creating a hole for the light fixture.

3. Follow the instructions on the light fixture kit or slide the cut end (not the plug end) of the cord through a 3/8-inch nut, then a washer, and finally feed it through the top and out of the bottom of the plunger head. (See Illustration.)

4. Feed the wire through the 3/8-inch thread rod, connected to the bulb socket. Separate the wires at the end and hook them around the positive and negative screws and tighten to hold in place.

5. Once the socket is ready, slide it up into the plunger's head, letting the 3/8-inch thread rod poke through the top. Then slide down the washer and nut already waiting on the wire and screw it tight.

6. Screw in a long slender 40-watt appliance bulb while pinching the ribs together, allowing access into the plunger's head.

7. Add the On/Off switch, plug it in, and turn it on, baby! *Plunge the night away*.

If you reuse light fixtures from old lamps found at thrift stores, you can save even more money. The plungers will cost $6 or $7 for a pair, and that is a saving beyond repair. Spending $7 on the plunger lights was a sweet deal, but trying to find a bathroom sink (even a used one) for less than $50 was pretty tough. So I decided to mix things up a little and use a chrome salad bowl from the dollar store, which cost, you guessed it, *one dollar*.

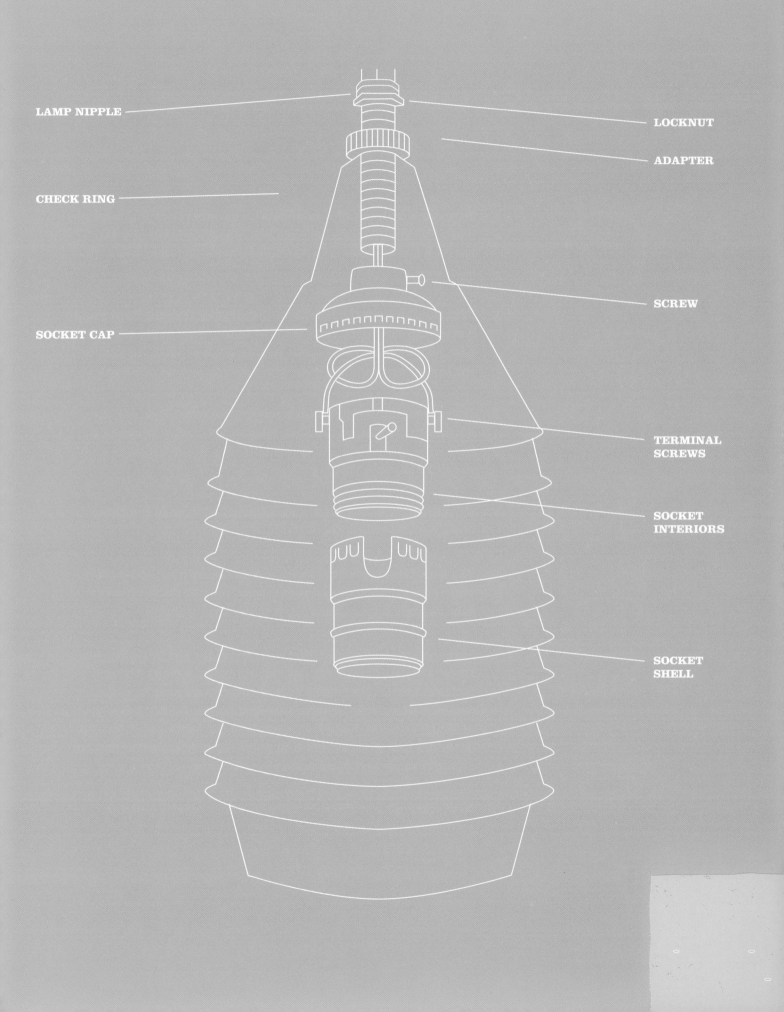

LAMP NIPPLE

CHECK RING

SOCKET CAP

LOCKNUT

ADAPTER

SCREW

TERMINAL
SCREWS

SOCKET
INTERIORS

SOCKET
SHELL

salad bowl sink

TOOLS YOU WILL NEED

Drill with 1 1/4-inch
hole saw bit

1 1/4-inch hole saw

MATERIALS YOU WILL NEED

Large salad bowl
Rubber washers
Silicone caulking

1. To make a sink out of a salad bowl, you must first find a salad bowl. I used an aluminum chrome-dipped bowl, but you can also use a bowl made of wood, hard plastic, ceramic, glass, or even steel.

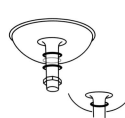

2. Find the center of the bottom of the bowl by turning it over and measuring the diameter. Mark the center. Then using a 1 1/4-inch hole saw bit (wood-metal bit), drill a hole in the bottom of the bowl. Then sand the hole with medium or fine sandpaper.

3. Use silicone caulking to seal around the new hole at both the top and the bottom of the hole. Slide in the rubber washers on both sides of the hole and screw down the drain flange around the sink tailpiece, making a tight seal.

4. Slide the sink tailpiece into the adjustable P-trap and tighten down the slip-joint nuts.

5. The sink I used was very light aluminum, so I had to seal the underrim with silicone adhesive caulking and place a heavy cement block on top, allowing it to dry overnight.

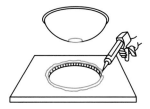

6. I also had to drill holes in the countertop for the water faucets (these are usually already cut into a porcelain sink). Using a 1-inch bit, I drilled two holes spaced according to my faucet's hot and cold water supply lines (threaded plastic tubes). After drilling the holes, I slid the faucet into the holes and tightened down the lock nuts to hold it in place. Then I reattached the hot and cold water and opened the shutoff valves.

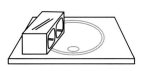

7. Now, wash off some lettuce, carrots, and tomatoes and mix yourself a salad in the sink!

BUDDHA-FALL KOI POND

In order to keep the Asian theme alive both inside and outside my house, I wanted to create a koi pond with a waterfall that had a nice tranquil sound and would help everyone relax in the bamboo-enclosed Zen garden.

I was working at the time for a client in the up-and-coming neighborhood where Vern lived. One of the houses across the street from my client's was having a slate stone roof replaced. The old tiles were stacked neatly along the curb and seemed abandoned and in need of a new home. As I was unloading some lumber for the job, I realized the tiles were still in pretty good shape and could be used quite nicely in place of stacked stones to build a retaining wall. Back at my house, I had started digging a hole in my backyard and was elated by the vision of the blue-gray slate shingles matching perfectly with a blue-gray statue of Buddha I had found at a flea market.

After finishing the job for my client, I packed my tools and all the unbroken slate shingles left on the curb. On my way home, I stopped at Vern's mailbox and left him a book called *Don't Sweat the Small Stuff* and my half-eaten egg salad sandwich (just for fun). Then I headed home to start building my Buddha-fall koi pond. This is how I did it in two days (even without Paige constantly reminding me that time is almost up).

The Buddha-Fall koi pond cost three days of intense labor, fifty-one mosquito bites, and three hundred and sixty dollars in materials, but having "front-roe" seats during the annual koi spawning season – priceless.

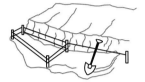

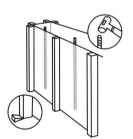

1. I dug a rectangular ditch 8 feet long, 3 feet wide, and 3 feet deep, making sure the sides and bottom were as straight and flat as possible by using string tied to stakes as a guideline.

2. Then I built a setting "form" (8 feet long, 4 feet high, and 3 1/2 feet wide) out of plywood and two-by-four wood spaced every 16 inches on center (like wall studs) on the outside of the plywood. Next, I placed the form at the back of the pond and extended it higher than the other walls to become a retaining wall high enough to create an elevated waterfall.

3. Using shims, I made sure the form was level. Then I drove rebar 4 feet long and 1/2 inch thick into the ground inside the 3 1/2-inch-wide channel of the plywood form to reinforce the concrete that I would pour and keep it from cracking.

4. Then I (should have) nailed 3-foot-long two-by-four wood to the form's frame (spaced 16 inches) at a 45-degree angle, skipping every other one to create support "legs" and keeping the form from bulging. (Since I didn't use quite enough support legs, the wall ended up having a slight wave to it.)

5. I mixed and poured the concrete into the channel of the form using a wheelbarrow, water hose, and shovel. I smoothed the top edge with a flat trowel and let it dry for twenty-four hours.

6. After the cement was dry I built a frame around the three other sides of the rectangle, using two-by-four studs spaced 16 inches on center. I then tacked a 14 foot x 14 foot pond liner made of 18-inch rubber to the top of the cement retaining wall, using cement nails. I made sure the liner lay flat on the ground floor and draped it over the three sides. I then tacked the liner to the frame using roofing nails, letting the liner fold and bunch in the corners.

7. After the liner was tacked, I began nailing the slate shingles to the (liner-covered) cement retaining wall using 1-inch cement nails. Starting from the bottom and working my way up by overlapping, I gently hammered the nails through the holes (which come predrilled on the slate shingles, which is nice) in the shingles, trying desperately not to break the slate stone shingles.

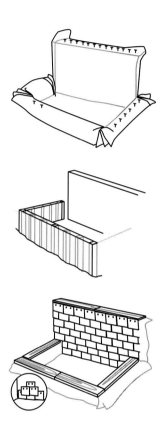

8. After all the tiles were in place, I covered the framed border edges with 1 inch by 6 inch pressure-treated lumber. Then I capped everything, including the slate-shingled wall (retaining wall), with copper flashing to hide the nail holes as well as to make a beautiful water-resistant edge cap that will develop a green patina with age.

9. I filled up the pond using a garden hose. After installing a water pump, I made a waterfall using a huge chunk of solid slate stone and concrete blocks. I used river rocks and a few leftover slate shingles to make a platform for the pump's recycling hose to rest under the Buddha, where that little statue could sit on top, giving it the illusion of a urinating Buddha, creating a waterfall that was simply Buddha-fall.

9. You can skip steps 2–5 by building a level wall using cement blocks and mortar. It's not cheaper but it is definitely easier.

To keep the "feng shui" swaying, I decided to bring the outdoors inside by using the same materials that I had used in creating my Zen garden to create a bamboo forest in my Phuket bathroom. The bamboo gave the room three-dimensional depth as well as a natural feeling of growth and harmony. The room felt like it was reaching out to your senses of sight, touch, and sound (especially before I fixed the running toilet, or should I say cascading waterfall). *The bamboo forest was cheap and easy to do, and that's what rocks about working with bamboo.*

BAMBOO FAUX-FOREST

bamboo faux-forest

TOOLS YOU WILL NEED

Table saw
Hammer

MATERIALS YOU WILL NEED

16 bamboo poles
Finish nails

It is so simple to make the bamboo faux-forest. Here is what you do:

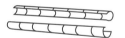

1. You will need about 16 bamboo poles, roughly 1 1/2 inches in diameter. Cut the bamboo poles the length of the ceiling height of the bathroom. Rip the poles in half using a table saw.

2. Nail the 32 halves of bamboo flat side down to the wall, using thin finish nails to hammer them in at the bamboo growth joints. This not only helps to hide the nails but also attaches the bamboo where it is the strongest.

The inspiration for the bamboo bathroom came from either the jungle fever or malaria I contracted building the koi pond. I really like this room; it gives a whole new meaning to the word "out" house.

BAMBOO "REACH-OUT" ROLL HOLDER

Since your new bamboo-enhanced wall will seem to reach out and touch you, I think you will enjoy having the toilet paper reaching out to be touched as well. I made a real simple toilet-paper holder by using a 1 1/2-inch-diameter curtain rod holder and about 6 inches of solid bamboo. Did I just say 6 inches of solid bamboo? I meant 7 1/2 inches of solid bamboo. Yeah, that's right. Actually, I'm not exactly sure how long my solid bamboo rod was, but just make it long enough to hold up a full roll of toilet paper without falling down on the job.

Here is how easy it is: Simply screw the 1 1/2-inch-diameter curtain rod holder to the wall. Next, slide in your new 8-inch shaft of bamboo (you see how these shaft measurements keep growing). Then, reach out and touch the soft fibers of the roll and then let them touch you.

TONGUE AND CHIC

One way to raise the value of your home is to cover your floors with hardwood flooring. Using tongue-and-groove flooring on your countertops and ceiling not only increases the value of your home but also raises a few eyebrows as well. It also begs the question "What can a material be used for, other than the purpose for which it was originally intended?" The answer to this question is "Quite a lot." In fact, tongue-and-groove flooring can be quite versatile as a hard surface material as well as offering several groovy uses for the tongue and groove that are simple and chic. You can create picture frames, shoji screens, countertops, doors, ceilings, and of course beautiful floors. Here's a couple of things I did with tongue-and-groove flooring.

This picture shows my excitement in finding out what the inside of bamboo looks like – when it's been turned into a fire-ant nest. *Ouch!!*

picture frames

TOOLS YOU WILL NEED

Miter saw or circular saw
Plate jointer
Clamps
Drill
Screws

MATERIALS YOU WILL NEED

Wood glue
1/4-inch Plexiglas
L-brackets
Tongue-and-groove flooring

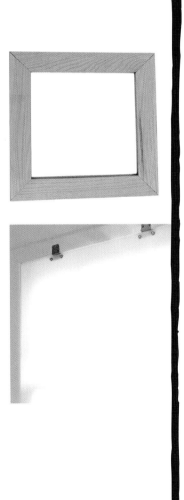

TONGUE-AND-GROOVE FRAMES

I created shoji screens for my bedroom window by using tongue-and-groove siding as my window trim molding. Facing the groove inside toward the window, I was able to slide the 1/4-inch Plexiglas into the 1/4-inch groove that held it in place, creating an extra layer of glass for insulation as well as an extra layer of visual diffusion for any private situations (*involving the use of tongue-and-groove*).

I'm sorry, but I couldn't resist. You see, it not only sounds good, it looks great, too.

Speaking of looking great, you can also use tongue-and-groove flooring or siding to make picture frames that can hold a glass mirror or a portrait. If you're like a few designers I know, then you're into creating "drama." To build a saucy frame, I suggest you use tongue-and-groove siding that is either 6 or 8 inches wide, made of a lovely wood such as cedar, cypress, or even old pine that is covered with old cracked paint, creating its very own drama. If you are a minimalist, I suggest you use tongue-and-groove flooring that is 3 or 4 inches wide and made of prefinished oak, maple, or Brazilian cherry. This will give your frame a clean, thin natural-looking border. *Whether it's old and cracked or clean and new, any tongue-and-groove flooring or siding will do to build a picture frame mirror that will reflect "the beauty" of being you.* Here is how you do it:

1. **Using a compound miter saw or a circular saw, cut a 45-degree angle on the tongue-and-groove flooring 12 inches from short side to short side.**

2. Place the four pieces together, making a square. Then mark with a thin leaded pencil a line across the 45-degree cut on both pieces that make a right angle corner.

3. Using a plate jointer, cut biscuit holes in each 45-degree cut, lining up the pencil mark with the center mark on the biscuit jointer.

4. Take two of the four pieces of the tongue-and groove and fill biscuit holes with glue and biscuits.

5. Use the table saw to cut the 1/8-inch Plexiglas into two 12-inch by 12-inch pieces.

6. Sandwich art or photographs between the two 1/8-inch Plexiglas pieces, making it now 1/4 inch thick.

7. Now slide the Plexiglas sandwich into the groove of one of the pieces of flooring with biscuits already inserted. Add the three other pieces of the flooring with biscuits with the holes and clamp together, making sure all corners are "square," 90-degree angles.

8. Wipe off excess glue and flip it over. Then place straight L-brackets in each corner. Using small screws, screw into place.

9. Flip over and hang on the wall.

TIP If you are making a frame for a picture or any kind of art on paper, use 1/8-inch-thick glass or Plexiglas (in place of the 1/4-inch mentioned above) and sandwich the picture between the sheets of glass. Insert the sheets into the grooves of the mitered-cut tongue-and-groove flooring.

Hopefully you can see not just your beautiful reflection in the mirror but that tongue-and-groove has enough tricks up its groove to keep you busy and probably get you tired with your tongue hanging out.

To match not only the Asian shoji screens but also the modern primitive design of my bedroom's furniture, I created bedside table lamps using Chinese placemats, fiberglass sheeting, and cutting (you guessed it) "grooves" into 12-inch-square pieces of ash. The placemats and fiberglass sheeting were bent and slid into the grooves to create several layers of shades for a lamp that could be either wall mounted or free-standing. These lamps were originally designed to include veneer in the place of the Chinese placemats creating tiered, veneered tai-lights. Now you can brighten up your home with a tai-light of your own. Just follow these simple directions:

1. Using a table saw or compound miter saw, cut one or two (depending on how many lamps you want to make) pieces of wood 10-inches by 12-inches, 3/4-inch thick.

2. Set the "fence" on the table saw 3/4-inch away from the blade.

3. Raise the blade 3/8-inch high to make a cut 3/8-inch deep.

4. With the long side against the fence, push the 10-inch by 12-inch piece through the table saw. Then switch and run the other long side through the table saw.

5. Make sure the blade has stopped. Then move the fence another 3/4-inch away from the blade. Make sure the distance or space between the first cut (or groove) and the edge of the wood is the same as the distance or space between the next grooves, which should be 3/4 inch.

6. Run both sides through the saw again. Now you should have four grooves. Move the fence away from the blade again until you have another 3/4-inch space between the last groove and the blade.

7. Run both sides through the saw one more time. Now you should have six grooves (three on each side) on the "face" of the 10-inch by 12-inch piece.

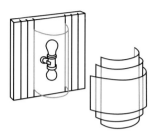

8. Find the center on the "back" of the 10-by-12-inch piece. Using a 1-inch hole saw or drill bit, drill down 3/8 inch. Then switch to a 3-inch bit and drill all the way through the board using the 1-inch hole center as your guide.

9. Now push the threaded rod of the two-bulb vertical lamp socket with wire first through the 3/8-inch hole on the "face." Tighten the nut from the "back" to the threaded rod. Use refrigerator lightbulbs as the light source.

10. Using a utility knife and a straightedge, cut fiberglass panels of "lacrolite" into smaller pieces. Cut clear 12x11 inches. Cut white 9x13 inches. Cut veneer (mahogany or birch) 6x15 inches. Then slide the panels into the grooves. Clear the panel closest to the bulb, then white the veneer.

All of these ideas are fun to try at home. The more experience you have thinking and playing "outside the box," the more creative you will become. I challenge you to start thinking about new ways that you can use old materials and push yourself to try new things.

Reinventing uses for common materials like tongue-and-groove flooring is a creative way to solve design problems resulting from the restrictions of a shoestring budget. Another way is to actually use the shoestring itself. For example, I reinvented uses for common materials but also common household items, hardware, and tools as well.

I created outdoor lanterns by drilling holes in old paint cans, which are illuminated with candlelight. I also made stylish stainless-steel planters for my "lucky bamboo" by simply using aluminum mud trays filled with pebbles and water instead of the usual joint compound. The most clever reinvention, however, was using chrome old-style hinges installed backwards to make a contoured custom fit seal to hold the white Plexiglas window screens snug tight inside the contoured shape of the window molding. I had to give myself two thumbs up on that one. If you think these are cool, wait until you read the painting sections and you see what I can do with a bleach bottle and a pair of women's panty hose.

Trading Uses: The outdoor lantern was a paint can, the planter was a mud tray, the paint bucket was a bottle, and the hinges are still hinges, only backwards.

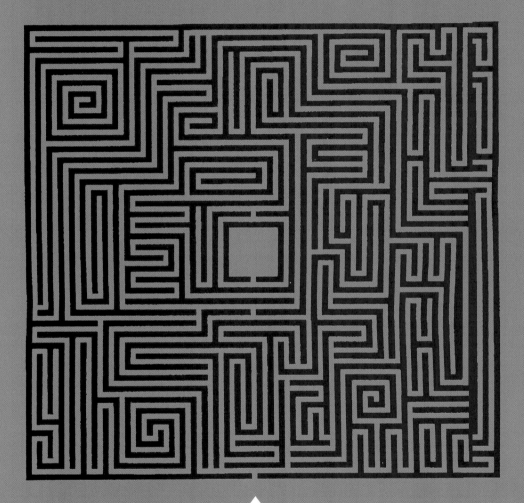

"If every problem has a solution, then every solution has a problem."

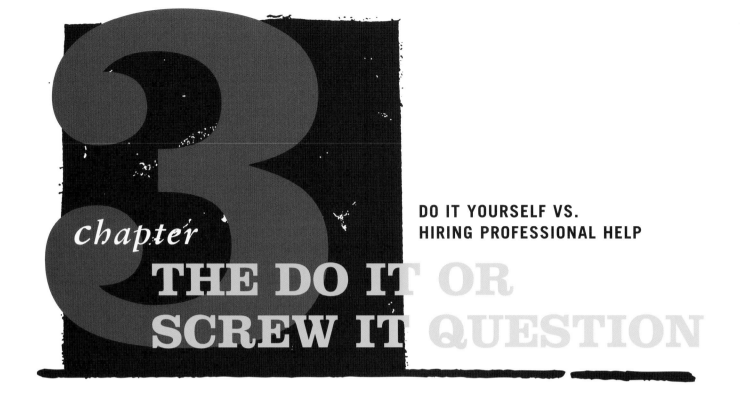

chapter

**DO IT YOURSELF VS.
HIRING PROFESSIONAL HELP**

THE DO IT OR
SCREW IT QUESTION

Learn, with Luck, While Earning a Buck

For most people, the big motivation for doing their own renovating and home repairs is to save money. I know that I've sure saved a great deal of money remodeling my house. I've even got my annual maintenance bill down to less than $400. In my corner of the South, the cost of replacing faucet washers and PVC pipe starts at about $70 — that is a certified plumber's minimum. A roofer will charge around $50 an hour, plus materials, to fix a leaky roof that you can repair yourself for about $4, including the tar. Flooring specialists charge $3 to $4 and up per square foot for installations.

Renovation Rap

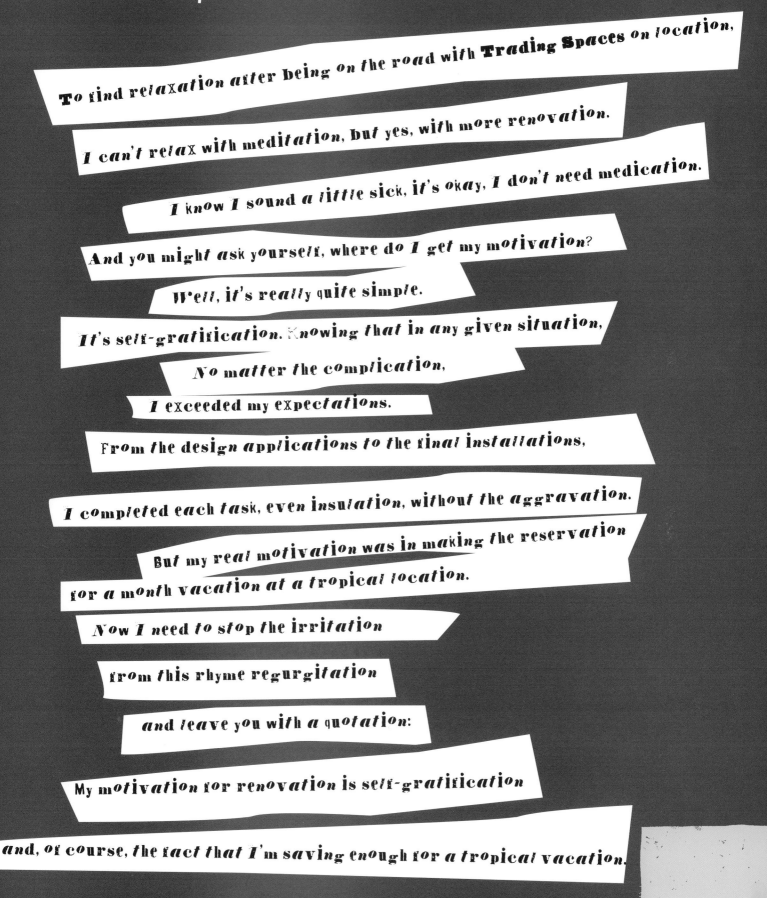

To find relaxation after being on the road with **Trading Spaces** on location,

I can't relax with meditation, but yes, with more renovation.

I know I sound a little sick, it's okay, I don't need medication.

And you might ask yourself, where do I get my motivation?

Well, it's really quite simple.

It's self-gratification. Knowing that in any given situation,

No matter the complication,

I exceeded my expectations.

From the design applications to the final installations,

I completed each task, even insulation, without the aggravation.

But my real motivation was in making the reservation

for a month vacation at a tropical location.

Now I need to stop the irritation

from this rhyme regurgitation

and leave you with a quotation:

My motivation for renovation is self-gratification

and, of course, the fact that I'm saving enough for a tropical vacation.

YOU MAY BE MANDY, RANDY, OR EVEN DANDY, BUT BEING HANDY HELPS

Now, granted you won't be as quick as a pro, but you can take as long as you want and you're still going to see a lot of cash left in your pocket.

Saving money, though, isn't the only reason to do your own home repair. The great feeling that comes with being truly self-reliant is a real kick. From swinging the hammer yourself to shedding your own blood, sweat, and tears, doing your own work feels good. Hopefully, too, you'll feel that existential rush that comes from figuring out why the toilet always makes that noise or why the door sticks only in the summer.

And don't forget that another advantage is simply getting the job done in the first place. Because, depending on how busy the building business is in your area, there is a good chance you'll have a tough time even finding a qualified "skillionaire" (professional) to take on a small job.

Finally, home repair offers divine enlightenment, a sublime form of education. You get paid to learn by saving money that you would have spent, you gain a better understanding of your home and how it works, and you face the personal challenge of working to a deadline and within a budget. Awesome!

TY'S tips

If it ain't broke, please **don't even try to fix it!**

As I've learned from my mother, we're all just human. We are all alike in many ways, but see ourselves as very different in our skills and abilities. Some of us see ourselves as naturally good with our hands and others as very good with our heads.

As a child, I was pretty much a guinea pig or lab rat for my mother, who as a psychology major would study people to find out how their minds worked. I remember one test in particular. First, my mother spread out a dozen or more geometric pieces of a puzzle on a glass table. Each piece was painted one of three colors and the object of the exercise was, within a certain time limit, to fit the right pieces symmetrically together in a perfect pattern. After spreading out the pieces, my mother turned over an hourglass and said, "Okay, you can start." Then she began writing in her journal. Now, here is the good part: Within seconds I had solved the puzzle. When I said, "Okay, I'm finished," my mother looked truly amazed. Of course, the second part of the test measured my communication and verbal skills, and my mother was equally amazed when I failed it miserably. I mean, I sucked. She found it to be quite interesting that I could be so good at a visual puzzle and so bad at a verbal puzzle. It was, in fact, puzzling.

But look, now I'm writing a book. To make a long story longer, I'm always puzzled when, say, an open-heart surgeon who thinks nothing of clamping an artery that's spewing blood like an open fire hose gets squeamish at the very thought of fixing a leaking faucet or valve. So many homeowners I've met, as well as many of my friends and family, are afraid to take on home repairs and renovations; you'd think they were doing their own taxes. They feel they lack the experience, confidence, or time to do it themselves, so they instantly call for backup. My friend Drea, for example, was ready to call in the National Guard for a running toilet. After I showed her the instructions on the back of a new flush kit, she ended up being out $7, saving about $70 that would have been paid to a plumber — not to mention learning, while earning, by doing the job herself.

In my world view, houses, like people, are quite simple to repair and maintain. We all get old eventually, and have accidents and injuries along the way — not to mention flus, common colds, and other unmentionables. So, instead of running to the emergency room every time we sneeze to have some specialist snap on a pair of latex gloves and wave a fresh tub of petroleum jelly, we learn to stock up on cough syrup, soup, and liquids (well, sometimes we lose a little more liquids than usual — we'll get to that in plumbing). Anyway, we learn how to nurse ourselves back to health. We learn about our bodies and save money on doctors' bills and insurance at the same time. Yet many of us, for some reason or another, still break into a cold sweat and dial 970-WE-FIX-IT, mumbling into the receiver, "I'll pay anything, just come quick — the house is bleeding." But wait until the bill: If you think Dr. Jelly with the latex glove is expensive, you'll really be sick when you see how much Mr. Fix-It charges.

So, my goal is to show you that you can do many repairs and renovations yourself and save those hard-earned ducats you've been paying to someone else. You'll learn how to examine your house from bottom to top (foundation to fixtures) with a certified home inspector and about hiring a professional or specialist for jobs too big or nasty to tackle alone. I'll talk about the good, the bad, and the ugly. I'll tell you to compare bids (before the contractor gives you the lumber, make sure he gives you a number) and how to prepare a contract (before he dims the lighting, get it in writing). I will try to communicate the lessons I've learned by doing it myself, hoping they inspire and reassure you. Some jobs are tougher than others, but when the going gets tough, the tough get going. Right? So, before you get going, possibly in the wrong direction, *have a plan you understand, have the will to learn the drill, and use your skills to pay the bills.*

START TO FINISH — WHAT'S THE PLAN?

Whether it's a game strategy, a mission statement, a wedding party, or a home renovation project, the first and most important step is drawing up a plan. The second most important thing is to make sure you can read and understand the plan.

Anyone who has watched *Trading Spaces* knows I've seen quite a variety of plans. Every decorator has his or her own personal style. Some plans are drawn like cartoons, with added humorous comments or insults; others are quite intricate, with several highly detailed views of elevations and even back views that a normal, geometrically challenged mind can find confusing. My personal favorite is what I call the napkin plan. It's not really a plan, but more of an idea scribbled down on a cocktail napkin while flying through turbulence in a plane. These plans, though probably intended to be simple, are even more difficult to decipher than ancient Egyptian hieroglyphics, especially when the ink mixes with spilled cocktail mixer. The first rule of construction: Before you start, make sure you can finish with a plan you understand. Plan WHO, WHAT, WHERE, WHEN, and HOW before you begin. The key to a good working plan is evaluation, preparation, and communication.

COMMUNICATION BREAKDOWN

If there is one certainty, it is that a serious lack of communication is going on out there. In this new age of technology, with cell phones and computers, with everyone chitchatting, sending e-mail with jpeg, pdf, and tiff attachments, and otherwise engaged in all that other www.org.net.dot.shiznit, you would think that simple communication between two people would be crystal clear. But the only animals on this planet who seem to understand each other are the ones who don't talk at all. But, hey, that's what makes life so interesting, right? Trust me, I've had my share of miscommunication, verbal and visual; not to mention the countless conversations I've had with designers about measurements and materials (or lack thereof) in preparation of projects, only to find complete confusion and chaos upon delivery. I believe that you and I (and, yes, maybe even designers) may have a vision. But only *you* can see that vision. Without clear communication, no one else can understand your plan, and, therefore, anyone else will probably hinder or harm rather than help. Because miscommunication is such a frequent factor in home repair projects, you must communicate your plans to everyone involved in the project — and vice versa if you've hired a "skillionaire" to do the job for you. Have made very clear WHO, WHAT, WHERE, WHEN, and HOW it is going to happen. And that means letting your family know before a job starts and they decide to leave, or you might end up trying to fix your marriage instead of the master bedroom.

Much has been said about family, such as "Blood is thicker than water," and "Friends can be picked, but family is forever." A personal favorite: "Marriage is happiness." My mom, family, says, "Marriage is marriage; happiness is how you make it." Well, I'm no family therapist, but my advice is: If you want your marriage to make it, you'd better make very clear the WHO, WHAT, WHERE, and especially WHEN and HOW of your home repair project or your marriage might not be! For example, I was working with my friend Rob (definitely Eager-Beaver). We were tearing the shingles as well as the rotten lumber off the roof of an old Victorian in preparation for new plywood. The owner was a client with several properties who thought of himself as quite the craftsman. He seemed to enjoy changing plans, designs, and projects that Rob (a certified draftsman and engineer) had labored over for many long nights and days. (I believe the homeowner was a specialist in the art of inheritance.) Anyway, on our productive days, he usually didn't hang around, but would stop in occasionally, having us stop one job, leaving it unfinished, to start another job. On one especially hot August evening, as we were finishing up and tying down the tarps over the freshly exposed roof rafters, he called us in to talk about the work ahead. As he showed Rob and me the different doors, windows, and knobs needing our immediate attention, he mentioned that his wife would be spending the weekend with him in the house and we were to work as usual, but to refrain from using profanity as much as possible. We were a little confused since we were unaware of his being involved with a woman, let alone being married.

Bright and early the next morning, as Rob, I, and a crew of carpenters began to untie the tarps protecting the interior of the house from the elements, the wind suddenly picked up. As the tarps blew away, the sky opened up, and lo and behold, lying there below us as exposed as the house without a stitch of roofing was a woman — now awake, wet, and very aware of her nakedness to a group of unknown men peering down from the rafters. After a few moments of staring up in awkward silence, the woman let out a sound very much like the screeching of brakes before a car accident, followed by some of the most vulgar profanity these ears have ever heard. (Trust me, I've heard a lot.) Of course, most of the profanity was vented at her soon-to-be ex-husband lying beside her. Having heard the thunder below and seeing the lightning above, we felt it best to retie the tarps and retire for the day. The homeowner, who luckily for us didn't also fancy himself as a lawyer, would long be seeking shelter from that storm.

So listen, do yourself a favor — no, better yet, do your entire family a favor — and schedule repair and remodeling projects when there will be a minimum of disruption; it just might save you from divorce. Remember, not everyone likes unexpected surprises. Just ask a few "underwhelmed" neighbors on *Trading Spaces*. However, a surprise makeover can definitely be a way to add a little spice in the bedroom. I would make sure, though, that you first have a well organized plan or the next surprise "redo" might be your marriage.

A PROJECT WITHOUT A PLAN IS LIKE A MAP WITHOUT A DIRECTION

In both cases, you're lost. The plan is a visual outline of the intended finished product. Many factors must be considered before arriving at a final plan for solving a design or project problem: budget, materials, structural, and deadline factors, not to mention the "fudge-it factor," which is the constant changes and unexpected surprises (Murphy's Law) that have to be "fudged" in order to complete a project. But having a well thought-out plan can usually anticipate and eliminate any unforeseen complications.

TIP Assess the situation before you start the renovation.

TIP Measuring twice and cutting once is a good way to cut down on the "fudge-it factor."

Repairing your home can be a long, hard road, but at least you can say it's your own asphalt!

MISTAKES

You see, even a seasoned professional can't fully anticipate human error. We, as humans, forget things, such as when Vern asked me to build him a headboard 10 feet high and 8 feet long. "No problem," I said. But I didn't realize that the headboard had to go up an interior staircase with an 8-foot ceiling height. Oops! I think we have a problem. So, I had to cut the headboard in half, leaving a "beautiful" rough-cut seam all the way through it. My point is, "S--t happens." It's an unwritten rule known as Murphy's Law. It is inevitable, but there are steps you can take to prepare for these inevitable unpleasantries. For example, in carpentry, there is an old, simple saying, "Measure twice, cut once." But because no home or project is the same, especially straight or level, there is always an unwanted surprise waiting in the dark for your arrival.

So, my advice for any carpentry project is: "Measuring twice is good advice, but when you're in a pinch, add an eighth of an inch." Even better is: "Add a width of a blade to the mark you've made, cut it long, and you can't go wrong." It totally sucks when you cut the last piece of trim, then nail it in place and spot a 1/2-inch gap, which you can caulk or be prompted to say, "Fudge it," and go back to the home improvement store to buy more trim. Returning, rebuying, and redoing is a constant "redoneit" factor that comes with every project. Most factors, such as budgets and materials, can be fairly easy to anticipate. But deadline and structural factors can require professional help and advice to make sure you can physically, financially, and structurally finish a project before you start. Hiring a home inspector is a good way to check out structural soundness of a project. *Expect the worst. Inspect it first.*

TY'S tips

Home inspectors are in the business of assessing the structural integrity of existing homes. These experts are usually hired by buyers during the purchase of a home. But they can also provide important insight on the need for repair. Since they don't make repairs, inspectors do not stand to gain by suggesting unnecessary work.

HOME INSPECTORS

I won't say too much about these guys because I don't recommend that you invite one over to your house to make you really dwell on your dwelling. Most of the time, I do believe "no news is good news," but when you're a homeowner, quite often only bad news seems to be delivered by plumbers, electricians, carpenters, and HVAC guys. But a home inspector will take you on a journey (no, not a tropical vacation) to places inside and outside of your house you never knew existed — some you'll wish you never found. You will become enlightened to the harsh reality of your home's structural condition, starting with the foundation, right up to the fascia. He (or she) can show you what's not safe or up to code, what should be done first, what are the telltale signs of water damage, termites, roof leaks, etc. Bottom line, a home inspector can save you money in the long run.

Don't be afraid to find out about the underworld of your house. Take a good look at the foundation walls down there in the basement. Get down on your hands and knees, and prowl the crawlspace. Check for crumbling concrete or mortar as well as loose blocks, bricks, or stones. Don't freak out over small stuff, but a large crack (1/4 inch or more wide) in the foundation that seems to be moving (widening and narrowing) or getting longer is a sign of a serious "settling" problem. Check the floors, doors, and windows above the crack and chances are they'll be out of square. (My own house has been "settling" for so long it's more than out of square — the flooring between supports of the foundation slopes like a skateboard ramp.) Now, while you're down there on your stomach with that flashlight in your hand and those spiderwebs in your hair, roll over onto your back to check the beams and joists for tiny holes and piles of sawdust, signs of carpenter ants, or tunnels, possible termite damage. Also look for dark stains on the wood, an indication of water damage.

Oh yeah, while you're still down there, check if the underside of the flooring is insulated. Trust me, it's well worth the trouble to staple up a little insulation; if your house has the same "character" as mine, it's not very well insulated and can get a little drafty. Actually the heart-of-pines flooring in my house was nailed directly to the joists, without a subfloor underneath it. Well, they don't build them like that anymore — praise the Lord!

My self-reliant attitude was shaped by my mother, who did almost everything herself and raised my brother and me alone — no small feat. It is imbedded in me that there is nothing I can't do myself (well, maybe a few things, such as open-heart surgery and giving birth — but hey, give me a manual and who knows?). I can think of a lot of reasons why you might not want to take on your own home repairs, but I personally have a real problem with paying someone else to fix a leak, build a deck, or replace a sink when I can do it myself, cheaper, faster, and without a kink.

That's right, I'll do it all myself — just as soon as I get my superhero costume back from the dry cleaner. Okay, I'm stretching the truth a bit. Let's just say that my goal is to take on any job myself and if it becomes too much to handle to call for backup. I'm stoked to say, though, that during my time in the three apartments in the warehouse and in the four years I've owned my house, I've not had to call in reinforcements. The smartest route, particularly if you are a beginner, is to take on the easy jobs and hire out the gnarly ones. In the words of Clint Eastwood, "Man's got to know his limitations." But, hey, there is no reason to sell yourself short. If you become an Eager-Beaver plumber and can't wait to sink your choppers into those waste-filled drainpipes, I say, "You go get 'em, stallion." On the other hand, if you're comfortable to be a Meager-Beaver, nibbling on occasion into installing a ceiling fan or pressure-washing the back deck, I'm right there with you, too. Either way, you'll save some cash, learn about your house, and acquire some tools — and hopefully gain confidence for the next project. Some words of caution: Don't be a Stupid-Beaver and hurt yourself trying too hard to do it yourself. Even a dam-building beaver knows when to say enough is enough!

BEAVER REALIZATION EVALUATION

This series of questions is designed to help you determine what level of skill you have in home improvement and repair. They will hopefully guide you in deciding on which jobs you can do and which jobs you absolutely should not do. Answer "yes" or "no" to each question. Depending on your final total of "yes" and "no" answers, you can determine if you are a Meager-, Eager-, or Reliever-Beaver. It's just for fun — and you just might become a better Believer-Beaver.

1. **Are You A Dusty/Rusty Beaver?** □Y/□N
You used to be pretty good with a hammer and wrench, maybe worked summer jobs that included some building or repair, but have since let your tools gather dust in the basement.

2. **Are You A Procrasta/Reader Beaver?** □Y/□N
You have read hundreds of books on building decks, boats, log cabins, garages, and so on, but have yet to start any project.

3. **Are You A Remote/Receiver Beaver?** □Y/□N
You have watched every do-it-yourself show on cable, hooked up your stereo to your TV to create "surround sound," but you still can't get your VCR to record.

4. **Are You A Wheezer/Sneezer Beaver?** □Y/□N
You have tried countless times to repair and remodel your home yourself, whether it be removing mold or mildew, or painting the walls. But before you even break ground, you break out in a rash of allergic reactions.

5. **Are You A Wheeler/Dealer Beaver?** □Y/□N
You could sell Girl Scout cookies to Girl Scouts and keep a low overhead, but installing a new header is a little over your head.

6. **Are You A Cleaner/Neater Beaver?** □Y/□N
You have simple, clean designs planned for your home, but the thought of the dust and clutter that comes with home renovation makes you reorganize your organizer.

7. **Are You A Closet/Faucet Beaver?** □Y/□N
You are right at home on the throne, sewer, or sink, or you're the grand flushmaster; your kingdom is the drain.

8. **Are You A Steeper/Leaper Beaver?** □Y/□N
You are gung-ho and willing to do anything thrilling, including hurting (or hurling) yourself.

9. **Are You A Damn It/Jamb It Beaver?**
□Y/□N You are a little impatient and live by the principles of "If it doesn't fit, make it" and "If it doesn't bend, break it."

10. **Are You A Busy Beaver?** □Y/□N Your list is full of things to do, and you could finish them all if you could stop time, too.

11. **Are You A Dream/Weaver Beaver?** □Y/□N
Your better half brings home the bacon, but can't fix the sink or the can.

12. **Are You A Preacher/Teacher Beaver?** □Y/□N
You know everything about everything. You are usually overconfident, overbearing, and leave everyone else just over it.

If you answered "no" to all the questions except #7, then you are definitely an Eager-Beaver and hopefully won't have to hire a plumber. If you answered "yes" to any or all the questions except #7 and #12, then you are a Meager-Beaver and will probably need a little help. But that's okay because after reading this book, you won't need to call a Reliever-Beaver. Every Beaver, though, has to know his or her limitations.

HERE IS A LIST OF HOME REPAIR JOBS AND THE APPROPRIATE LEVEL OF HOMEOWNER EXPERTISE

Jobs for Meager-Beavers
(the beginners)

- Drywall and plaster — repairing small holes
- Unclogging drains, fixing running toilets and leaky valves
- Painting, staining, applying polyurethane and varnish
- Prepping — sanding and caulking
- Replacing windowpanes
- Installing subfloors

Jobs for Eager-Beavers
(the confident)

- Drywall and plaster — repairing large holes and sheet installation
- Replacing windows
- Installing ceramic tiles and hardwood (tongue-and-groove) flooring
- Installing copper and PVC pipe
- Building a deck

Jobs for Reliever-Beavers
(the "skillionaires")

- Replacing windows and doors
- Super-serious drain cleaning
- Installing galvanized pipe (gas line)
- Working on high or steep roofs
- Dealing with the circuit-breaker panel or fuse box
- HVAC (air conditioning)

HIRING A HANDYPERSON

What's required before they get hired?

PROS AND CONS

Now, before I devote the rest of this book to helping you handle your own repair projects, let's explore the process of choosing and paying for the right professional. Whether you lack the time, experience, or persistence, we all eventually have to hire a certified specialist. Be it a subcontractor or a contractor, some jobs require a pro. But the real trick is telling the pros from the cons.

The Good, the Bad, and the Ugly. We've all heard of the horrors of hiring the wrong help. *They take twice as long at thrice the price, leave the job unfinished but seemed so nice!* Hiring good help is never easy. The best way to find the best help is through word of mouth. Ask your neighbors, friends, and coworkers who they've used for renovation and repair projects, and don't forget to quiz them about their level of satisfaction with the work.

Dialing a number you find in the phone book is like gambling in Vegas, but when it comes to home repair, it can be a lot more costly! You have to ask yourself, "Am I feeling lucky?" And with a little luck, you might actually find good contractors, but chances are they're Busy-Beavers because business is good and they're in demand. So, you'll have to wait for a break in their schedules.

I've met quite a variety of pros and cons over my years in the business. Some have no business being in the business, and some are out of business because they're good at bad business.

The Good (the Overachiever-Beaver). There are some contractors who are very good at their jobs. In fact, they're actually too good. They're perfectionists, and as perfectionists, they're not happy until the job is overworked, over-budget, and over-deadline. But if you can handle the wait and the budget, they will finish the job and make things perfect — if there is such a thing.

The Bad (the Cheaper-Deceiver Beaver). There are also contractors who are very bad at their jobs. They deceive you by telling you that they can do an excellent job at a very low price, known as underbidding. They offer a price so low that it seems too good to pass up. The only problem is they usually hire very hungry or inexperienced workers. As a result, these cheap laborers can create all kinds of problems that may have to be fixed by someone else. And that work won't be so inexpensive.

The Ugly (the Bull-Believer Beaver). Well, there is the good, the bad, and, yes, even the ugly. Now, these guys actually might be easy on the eyes, and seem charming and intelligent, but they're really the devil in disguise. They'll have you believing they're the best in the biz. Then, surprise, you realize that you're being taken for a ride. These contractors are notorious for telling you "these things take time," then showing up four hours late to work only half a day.

There are hundreds of stories out there too gut-wrenching to tell. They all start with a hopeful homeowner and end with a huge bill. But hiring help doesn't have to hurt. To prevent your home repair project from becoming *Poltergeist 3,* there are steps you can take to make the hiring-help process less prone to hassles and assaults on your wallet.

Prepared to Repair. Is the person ready to make the commitment? We've all been in relationships that started out good, went bad, then became downright ugly. When choosing the right person for your renovation repairs, ask yourself first, "How much does he (or she) care?" Is the person aware that all is fair in love and home repair? Did he just come out of a long-term relationship? What was the repair? Is the handyman relationship free, except for your repair? Or is he a two-timing tool man who always keeps a spare? Is he willing and able to commit full-time? Is he aware that during the repair he might have to compromise? Is he too busy? Is there a better time? Does he mind putting something in writing? What is his story? What is his sign?

Well, you get the idea. Ask a lot of questions. Not just about past work, but also about personal life. Is he married? Does he have kids, mouths to feed? Is he a beer-drinking bachelor who likes to work high on weed?

REPAIR QUESTIONNAIRE: To Hire or Fire

PLEASE ANSWER THE FOLLOWING QUESTIONS BELOW:

PAST PROJECTS

1a What was your most recent home repair project? ....

1b How did it go? ....

....

STATUS

2 Will you be doing the work yourself or just supervising? ....

3a How long have you been doing this kind of work? ....

3b Is it your specialty? ....

4 How long do you think it will take? ....

5 How soon can you get started? ....

6a Can you do all of my repairs? ....

6b If not, can you recommend someone for the repairs you cannot do? ....

7a How long have you been self-employed? ....

7b Who did you work for before you went solo? ....

8 Do you mind signing a contract that will include both start and completion dates as well as an itemized bid? ...

9a What are your work hours? ....

9b Will you be working on other jobs while working on this job? ....

PERSONAL INFORMATION

10a Do you have a family? ....

10b Where are you from originally? ....

11a Am I asking too many questions? ....

11b Do you find me annoying? ....

11c Really? ....

11d Why? ....

11e Do you like anchovies? ....

ESSAY PORTION

YES, I DO HAVE CERTAIN PREFERENCES, AND ONE OF THEM IS I ALWAYS NEED REFERENCES

The right person for the job will always provide you with references. If he (or she) doesn't, it should be your first warning that he may not have done valid work before, or that he is trying to hide something. You don't want a handyman with a skeleton in his closet that could cost you time and money.

Once you've gotten the references, don't hesitate to call and check them out. Many people make the mistake of not checking the references they get. This is a *big* mistake! You need to know as much as possible about the good, the bad, and the ugly before the crew starts demolishing, I mean *fixing*, your house.

BASIC QUESTIONS TO ASK

Think of yourself as being set up on a blind-date in two days and you need all the information about the mystery person in the shortest time possible. Ask all the important questions — this could be the beginning of a lengthy relationship. Don't you want to know if he (or she) has got what it takes?

1. WHAT KIND OF WORK DID THE HANDYMAN DO? DID IT BEAR ANY RESEMBLANCE TO YOUR PROBLEM (IT HELPS TO KNOW THE SPECIFICS, BECAUSE YOU WILL FIND OUT A LITTLE ABOUT WHAT NEEDS TO BE DONE ON YOUR OWN HOME)?

2. WOULD YOU RECOMMEND HIM? WHY?

3. HOW LONG DID IT TAKE HIM?

4. DID YOU SET A DEADLINE? IF SO DID HE STAY WITHIN IT?

5. DID THE FINISHED PRODUCT TURN OUT THE WAY YOU HOPED IT WOULD?

6. WAS HE NICE? (SEEMS NUTS, BUT YOU ARE GOING TO BE SPENDING A LOT OF TIME WITH YOUR HANDYMAN, SO THIS IS A VALID QUESTION.)

7. DID HE LISTEN TO YOUR IDEAS AND TAKE THEM INTO CONSIDERATION?

You can even ask questions about whether or not he has other responsibilities, and other questions that will help you determine if he has compelling reasons to stay on the job and handle your project with care.

Keep in mind that handymen will most likely give you the names of people who are certain to give rave reviews, so you need to take some of the claims made by references with a grain of salt.

DO YOU MEASURE A HANDYMAN'S PERFORMANCE IN INCHES OR SQUARE FEET? STATE LICENSES, CREDIT REPORTS, THE BBB, AND PORTFOLIOS

THE STATE HAS GOT THE DATE FOR YOU

Checking to see if someone is a licensed contractor is the easiest way to find out the validity of his (or her) work. Requirements for state licenses can be very strict in order to protect you from any Tom, Dick, or Mary working on your home. Check to see if your state licenses contractors; not all states do. In a state that doesn't license, you run the risk of getting a contractor with no formal training. When licenses are not required, anyone can call himself a general contractor. The scary part is he could know less about construction than you. The blind leading the blind is no way to go in repairing a house!

States without licensing requirements tend to be overrun with inexperienced, untrained, and sketchy characters passing themselves off as qualified contractors. They can sound knowledgeable, look legit, and even have references, but that doesn't mean they're the real McCoys. Choose wisely — your house and your checkbook depend on it.

Worst-case Scenario: They take the money and run. It happens. Start asking friends and neighbors about construction or repair work they've hired out to get done on their homes and the bet is you'll be hearing some haunting tales.

Size Doesn't Matter. There is an old saying that goes, "It's not the size of the hammer, but the power behind it." Well, depending on who you ask, this may be debatable. Generally speaking, when it comes to contractors, I believe that size doesn't matter. The big companies are always busy, this is true. But the guys doing the actual work aren't the guys you talked to. On the other hand, the small independents are hungry for work, but hungry doesn't help when the job goes berserk! Depending on your job, budget, and time frame, you're better off with mid-size most of the time. These guys have most often worked for the big guys, then branched out on their own. They're not as big as they come, but they're eager to grow and so are invested in doing a good job. *They usually are competent and committed to prices not necessarily low. But they are reasonable, reliable, and people good to know.*

GET A NUMBER

Get a number before the handyman brings you the lumber. We've all been swept up in the excitement of a new relationship. Nervous and awkward, we let down our guard. *So, before you start spending and pretending that you're livin' large, find out first what the hell he's going to charge.*

A good contractor will usually give out free estimates. Estimates, or bids, are beneficial to you, the homeowner, for several reasons. First, they can start a bidding war. Second, these bids will give you a good idea of what it will cost you in materials, labor, and time, just in case you decide to tackle the job on your own. Be sure to get an itemized bid, separating out the materials (usually by the square foot) and labor (usually by the hour). Then, compare the prices, checking to see if the markup price is consistent and what the actual price is compared to the estimate.

How to Break Down a Bid in Four Easy Steps

1. **Instincts and trust:** Bids are not just about numbers. You have to get a feel for your contractor. Does he look you in the eye when you are talking? Does he listen to what you have to say? Does he understand what you want and is he willing to support you or at least show you a better way to do something? Is he helpful? If you get a bad feeling about a handyman who comes into your house, then your sixth sense is telling you that there is something wrong. Always follow your instincts. Remember, this is a relationship. Look for qualities in your handyman that you would look for in your man.

2. **Separate costs:** Materials, labor, and hidden charges. First of all, you want an itemized bid. This allows you to see exactly what you're paying for. Materials and labor should be the first things you look at.

    Materials: Everything from nuts and bolts to lumber and paint is part of the materials you're going to be paying for. Always remember that the prices will be marked up, so do a little research and call around to lumberyards, hardware stores, and home improvement supply companies to compare prices. You may be able to find a better price, or you may find out that the contractor's prices are not as bad as you thought. This is also a good way to learn more about your house and become more involved. The more involved you are, the more likely you are to have the job get done the way you want. Lumber, for example: Lumberyards can give you estimates if you know the measurements and amounts of wood you will need. Check around at a few places to get an average and compare it to the price your contractor quoted you. You can then negotiate with him with the knowledge and evidence to back you up.

3. **Padding:** How much of a markup should you expect from a contractor? You are going to be looking at a margin of about 15 percent to 30 percent — over that and he can forget it unless he is the last contractor on Earth.

4. **Goldilocks:** Picking the perfect bid. Take into account the cost, quality of materials, and background information on the contractor.

GET IT IN WRITING — BEFORE HE DIMS THE LIGHTING

So, you've got his digits and done the background check. His numbers match up and you're ready for the next step. *Before you uncork the bottle of wine, write up the contract that you both should sign.*

This contract is a working agreement involving both parties — the homeowner and the contractor — stating what job is to be done, when it should be started and completed, and the approximate price. This ensures that you, the homeowner, have recourse to legal action if services are not rendered as written. And this contract protects the contractor from you, the homeowner, adding new and different jobs not mentioned prior to starting the project. Believe me, it happens. This means that you can finally celebrate your new working relationship because, in a way, you've just gotten married. Congratulations!

HOLD THE CHECK — GET MUCH RESPECT

PAY HALF UP FRONT

In order to get the job started, materials will need to be purchased. In my experience, it is customary to pay half of the estimated price up front.

TIP Do not write that final check until you have completed a thorough walk-through with the contractor, asking questions about the work. Make sure that you have a punch list. This is a list of unfinished or small jobs that must be completed before the contractor and crew leave your home forever. If you pay in full before the jobs are finished, you can bet your asphalt that they will hit the highway, hit the bank, and leave you with a ditch instead of a driveway. Money can be quite a motivator. Money is power, and more power to them. *But don't give them the power until they finish the shower!*

A HANDY SUMMARY FOR HIRING HELP

1. Be wary of walk-ups; instead, rely on word of mouth. Ask your friends and neighbors who they hired and how the job went.

2. Ask for references. Call the other clients. Get the dirt on the dude.

3. Ask lots of questions. How long has the contractor been in business? Is he committed? Is he working on other jobs?

4. Get several bids. Make sure that each bid is itemized by materials, labor, and time.

5. Get it in writing. Have him sign a contract with both a start and completion date. Before he starts, make sure that he will finish.

6. Don't pay him in full before he is finished. Make a punch list of work to be completed before final payment is made.

LET THE AIA DO THE WORK

A contract's main role is to protect you. It could be your best witness if you wind up in court about an unfinished job. You want to use the best contract that you can get your hands on, and if you don't want to create one yourself, the AIA (American Institute of Architects) contract is your best bet. Copies are widely available. The AIA has offices all around the United States, or you can print the contract off the Internet site *www.aia.org*. If you wish, you can make up your own customized contract by adapting the AIA contract.

Your handyman will have a contract of his own specifying what he is and is not liable for and detailing exactly what he will be doing. If you pick materials instead of going with what he suggests, he can write into the contract that he is not liable for wear and tear on the materials. After he is through with a job, the upkeep is up to you.

BEFORE YOU EVEN START, MAKE SURE THE CONTRACTOR IS GOING TO FINISH

Time limits are your best guarantee that the contractor will finish the job. As the time runs out he begins to lose money, and if he doesn't make the deadline, he could end up in a position of paying you to work.

Time limits can be worked into a contract. This guarantees you the focus and attention of your handyman. Set deadlines and penalties for not making deadlines. This protects you from having work that is half done sitting around for weeks while your money is helping to fund other projects.

Okay, you're ready for the corkscrew.

GO IT ALONE

Now that you have all you need to know to hire the right person to help you with the big jobs, I'll spend the rest of the book inspiring and helping you to do many of the small jobs yourself. Hopefully, you're strapping on your tool belt at this very moment and saying, "Bring it on!"

"Tools are instruments made by man that return the favor."

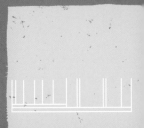

chapter

THE BEST TOOLS AND MATERIALS

TY'S TOOLS

A Tool: Guy's Best Friend (Everyone Can Use One)

A job worth doing, so the saying goes, is a job worth doing well. And the key to doing a job well is having the right tools for the job — and, of course, knowing how to use them. Power tools, in particular, can make a job seem like a dream . . . or turn the dream into a nightmare, sending you off to the hospital emergency room. Tools can be lots of fun, but they aren't things to play around with unless you really know how to use them. But if you do know how to use them, man, are they amazing. Am I right, ladies?

Tools come in all sizes: big, small, battery-operated, or air-powered. Some are required for certain specific jobs that you'll do only very rarely; these you should try to borrow, or rent by the day or hour. Other tools are necessary to have on hand. Some are needed for big, involved jobs, and others are needed just for a quick fix. *I will help you put together an essential tool kit to do-it-yourself with no doubts. I'll share with you the tools I frequently use and can no longer live without.*

Just as you should have a first-aid kit for injuries to yourself (or your family), so you should also have a supply of tools on hand for home repair "emergencies." This Can-Do-It kit should consist of a few great tools that "can do" more than just one job. So, without further ado, here are my essential Can-Do-It tools — please turn the page:

Speed square: This three-in-one tool will help you measure, mark, and check angles up to 90 degrees. It can also serve as a saw guide to cut 45- or 90-degree angles with a circular saw or a jigsaw; the overhanging edge must be held firmly against the edge of the workpiece.

Claw hammer: Heavy-duty 24-ounce model is one of my favorite tools — great for pounding and prying.

Needle-nose pliers: This gripper, with a built-in wire cutter is used in tight spaces or for delicate work. Handy for working with electrical wires.

Channel-lock pliers: This tool's special feature is that the jaws remain parallel no matter how wide open, giving a great grip on any shape. A favorite for plumbing work — to grab pipes and other round objects.

Chalk line: Chalk-coated string is pulled out and "snapped" against a surface to mark a long straight line. The string can also serve as a leveling line, and can suspend the tool's body for use as a plumb bob.

Torpedo level: This short version of a carpenter's level lets you check for level or plumb. At 9 inches long, it's especially good in tight spaces and short enough to be kept in your tool belt. Often magnetized on one edge for hands-free leveling of metal objects.

Tape measure: It's a must-have, so fork out the bucks for a quality one with a solid locking mechanism.

Handsaw: A short one with combination teeth is useful for fast cutting when the "power" of a circular saw isn't needed.

5-in-1 tool: It's literally five tools in one: putty knife, crack opener, scraper, paint roller cleaner, and even screwdriver.

C-clamp: An extra pair of hands, and your best buddy on many jobs. C-clamps come in many sizes, and will hold objects firmly to a table or sawhorse while you work on them; lock pieces tightly together while you fasten them or glue sets; or keep a saw guide perfectly in place.

MADE IN USA
U.S. PAT. 452454

All the tools in the Can-Do-It kit are great because they're so versatile. Most of them will even fit into your tool belt, so they'll always be close at hand.

Now, for jobs where you need more power, the one tool that you'll reach for time and time again is a power drill. No tool kit is complete without a power drill, corded or cordless, and a selection of bits.

DO YOU KNOW THE DRILL?

DRILLS 101, AN INTRODUCTION

Drills are rated by chuck size, or the biggest diameter bit that fits. The most versatile sizes are 3/8 inch and 1/2 inch. A 3/8-inch model is a good "starter" drill. Even if you move up to a heavy-duty 1/2 inch, you'll still find yourself reaching for your trusty 3/8 inch more times than not. Speed and power capabilities for corded drills are indicated by amperage; for cordless drills, by number of volts of battery power. Now, while a higher power rating (amps/volts) lets you rev up and drill faster with greater torque (vroom, vroom!), the more powerful the drill, the heavier it is, and the more strength you need to control it. This can mean serious muscle ache if you'll be using it all day long.

Get a variable-speed model — by varying your pressure on the trigger, you control the drilling speed. Different materials need to be drilled at different speeds. Harder woods, for example, should be drilled slowly to prevent burning or splitting. And when you're driving screws, a slower speed helps keep the bit from flying off (yee-ouch!) or stripping the heads. Also, by slowing down, you can be sure not to drill or drive a screw deeper than you intend.

With a reversible drill, you can easily back the bit out of a hole you've just drilled, as well as loosen or remove screws. And I love the convenience of a keyless chuck. A quick flick of the wrist and a new bit is installed — no more groping around for a chuck key (which is always AWOL when you need its duty). On the flip side, a keyless chuck's grip on the bit will never equal that of a keyed chuck — a real drawback when working with a large-diameter bit or drilling into hard material such as concrete.

TY'S tips

A one-dollar bill is exactly 6 inches long and can be used in a pinch for measuring.

THE DRILL FOR DRIVING SCREWS

When is a drill not a drill? When it's a screwdriver, of course. "Screwing your-self" isn't a pleasant home-repair thought. But getting screwed can sometimes be a good thing, especially if your other choice is getting nailed. Most people prefer the speed and accuracy of a power drill to drive screws, compared to driving nails with a hammer. Screws are good for avoiding nasty hammer blows, and preventing chips or cracks in plaster, drywall, and other finished surfaces. Not to mention, if you do screw up with a screw, simply switch your drill to reverse and out comes the screw, easy as pie. Try doing that with a nail! So, break out the screwdriver bits for your drill and away you go.

There are several types of specialty power screwdriving drills available to screw-it-yourselfers, such as a drywall screw gun, with a clutch to prevent driving screws too deep. But generally speaking, a reversible drill is about as tasty as a tool can get for use as a powerful screwdriver. *It feels so good in your hand that you don't mind screwing up.*

Here are some tips for using a drill as a power screwdriver:

TIP For work on hard woods, which can split when driving in a screw, or for bigger jobs that wear you out from applying constant pressure on the drill, start by making a pilot hole. A pilot hole is drilled with a bit slightly smaller than the screw that you plan to use, allowing the screws to be driven more easily with better results. For not-so-delicate work, you don't have to bother with a pilot hole — as long as you've got some muscle.

TIP For power screwdriving, using Phillips-head screws instead of slotted or flathead screws means less chance of the bit slipping off the screw. For bigger jobs, you might want to get square-head screws, also known as Robertson-head, and the matching screw-driver bit. The bit gets a really solid seat in these screws, holding the screwheads even better than with Phillips-heads.

TIP Try not to let the bit slip because it could strip and destroy the screwhead. But if it does slip, try to finish off at a slower speed. If the head is stripped, remove the screw by putting your drill in reverse (or use pliers) and try another screw.

TIP Be careful not to screw your finger when using a power screwdriver. To keep from shredding your digits, hold the screw in place with a magnetic driver bit, placing the screw on the bit before drilling. This works best for square-head screws, with Phillips-head screws coming in second. (Trust me, getting those little metal splinters really sucks.)

1

2

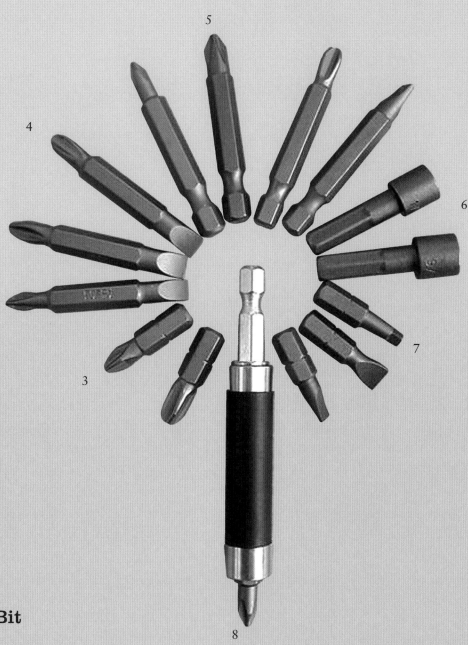

Bit by Bit

1. If you're in a hurry, this bit holder lets you change screwdriver bits and special hex-head drill bits without involving the drill chuck.

2. This adjustable combination bit makes a multilayered hole in one shot: It drills a pilot hole for the screw's threads and a hole for the shank. Then, it makes a wider, angled hole to sink the screwhead below the surface, and, if you drill deeper, a cylindrical hole to be filled with a wood plug or putty to hide the screwhead.

3. A small Phillips-head bit comes in handy for delicate work using smaller screws, such as installing hinges on a cabinet.

4. The two-in-one Phillips-head/flat-head combo bit slots right into the drill chuck.

5. A standard Phillips-head bit is the "original" power screwdriver.

6. A nut-driver bit holder essentially turns your drill into a power wrench, allowing you to tighten nuts, bolts, or hex-headed screws.

7. A square bit is used on square-head (Robertson) screws, which are less likely to strip or slip than Phillips-head or slot-head screws.

8. This magnetic bit holder has an extension sleeve, and is used to drive in longer screws without them wobbling and possibly flying off at an angle. Insert the screw onto the end of the bit, and slide the extension sleeve over the bit and screw to keep the screw going straight in.

TIPS AND TRICKS TO DRILL WITH SKILL

Generally speaking, we all have drilled and screwed. Some do it better, some do it worse. Some have been doing it longer, and have learned different tricks and techniques that make it as painless as possible. I'm not saying that I'm particularly "gifted" when it comes to the subject, but I know the drill and have learned how "not to get screwed."

TRICKS — OR, BITS ON BITS

Some do it, then redo it, and some shouldn't do it at all. Some really like doing it with a quick-changing variety of different tips and bits.

- Protect your eyes when you're operating a power drill — wear safety goggles. I can't drill this in enough: power tools = safety goggles. Your vision will thank you.

- If you've made a pilot hole that's just a bit too small, you don't have to go to a bigger bit. You can cheat by moving the drill around slightly as you drill, carving out a bigger hole. But be careful when using small-diameter bits; they can snap.

- If you need to drill a very small pilot hole — especially in soft wood — and you don't have a tiny drill bit, a finishing nail can save the day: Just snip the head off the nail and use the shank as a drill bit.

- Did you know that a drill can be used for much more than just drilling holes and driving screws? There are a number of attachments you can get to transform your drill: A mixing bit lets you turn a dusty bag of mortar, grout, or joint compound into the perfect mix. A variety of sanders can be chucked into your drill, such as a flap sander, or a sanding drum or disk. Other attachments include wire brushes and wheels, different-shaped rotary rasps and files, and grinding wheels.

- Look into getting some accessories that expand your drill's versatility. A right-angled drive head or a flexible shaft lets you use the drill in areas too tight to fit the entire tool.

DRILLING METAL (TAKES QUITE A BIT)

Sometimes screwing with your wood is just practice for a more challenging drill: metal. Steel, in particular, can be pretty tricky. And if you're not even making a dent, you may be dealing with hardened steel. Give up now because you won't penetrate. Things made of hardened steel, such as locks, are meant to be drill-proof. You'll find drilling through the soft metals, such as aluminum and copper, to be much easier going. Look into buying special bits for the type of metal you're thinking of giving a drilling.

Note: Keep a little motor oil handy for when things eventually get smoking hot. Drip a bit onto the spot you're drilling to prevent your bit from overheating.

Here are some cool tips for drilling hot bits through metal:

TIP 1 Always use a corded power drill when drilling metal. This job takes too much juice for a cordless drill — unless you're dealing with a material such as thin sheet metal.

TIP 2 If you don't have a variable-speed drill, now is the time to get one, since you'll want to slow down the bit to make big holes in metal. You can speed up again for small holes.

TIP 3 Forget the convenience of a keyless chuck: When drilling metal, you want the strength of a keyed chuck. Turn the key in two (or all three) chuck keyholes to guard against slipping.

TIP 4 Get off to a good start. To prevent a bit from skating on metal, give it a start point by making a small dent with a center punch. (On soft metal, tapping a nail may do the trick.)

TIP 5 If you're having trouble getting through the metal, start off with a smaller bit, then move up to the desired bit size.

TIP 6 Metal tends to dull bits, so have extras on hand — or be prepared to sharpen bits when necessary.

LOOK MA, NO CORD!

Oh, the joys of a cordless tool! It's so nice not to have to hunt for outlets and drag around extension cords (which often seem to have minds of their own), not to mention untangling yourself from them when you're trying to work. Cordless tools are great in remote locations: outdoors, in attics, up on ladders, in crawlspaces, etc. On the flip side, corded tools don't run low on juice just when you're at a critical point. Nobody likes a tool that can't finish the job (if you know what I'm saying). But there's a solution to this: Quality cordless tools come with a spare battery and a one-hour charger. Extra batteries are available, but they ain't givin' them away!

On *Trading Spaces* I have access to lots of cordless tools, everything from a circular saw to a reciprocating saw. I even have a battery-operated portable finish and framing nail gun. I have to admit that I save a chunk of time not having to deal with tons of extension cords or find available outlets. But for some jobs that require constant thrusting power, you need a tool with a good old-fashioned power cord since corded tools typically give you a steadier flow of power and more bang for your buck, torque-wise. For example, if you are drilling or cutting through hard metal, brick, or concrete, I definitely recommend using a corded tool.

A power tool, whether it has a cord or is cordless, makes repairing and remodeling easier. But for your most-used tools, such as drills, why not both? Having the option of using a corded or cordless drill is fantastic, but having the option of using both makes drilling even faster. And who doesn't like a good fast drilling?

To provide you with the power and performance to tackle almost any task, I recommend ten tasty tools that any screw-it-yourselfer or skillionaire pro should not be without.

TY'S TOP TEN POWER TOOLS

 1. Cordless drill

 6. Reciprocating saw

 2. Circular saw

 7. Jigsaw

 3. Compound miter saw

 8. Electric planer

 4. Orbital sander

 9. Finish nailer

 5. Table saw

 10. Belt sander

Saw Blades

There are all kinds of specialty blades for cutting wood with circular, miter, and table saws that you may want for more serious woodworking or finish carpentry. But for general wood cutting, just go for the basics listed below. As a general rule, a blade with fewer teeth gives a faster (but rougher) cut.

For the cuts that you'll need in home repairs — against the grain (crosscutting) or with the grain (ripping) — get a carbide-tipped combination blade. Compared to steel teeth, carbide teeth will give you many more miles of cutting before they need to be sharpened.

A plywood blade is good for cutting manufactured panels. It has many small teeth that cut down on splintering and are designed not to get jammed up with the glues in panel materials such as plywood and particleboard.

1. CORDLESS DRILL

My favorite is an 18-volt or 24-volt model. This drill packs a lot of power while being extremely portable. It's great for quick bit changes, and features a torque control that eliminates the stripping of screws.

2. CIRCULAR SAW

No carpenter worth his (or her) tool belt goes anywhere without his circular saw. It's one of the true workhorses of the work site. For home repair, it comes in handy for all kinds of cuts in many types and sizes of materials. The circular saw is versatile — quick adjustments let you set the blade to different depths and angles. It's great for making quick cuts, such as lopping off the end of boards; used with a guide, it can make precision cuts. And with the right specialty blade, you can cut almost any material — including brick, concrete block, metal, ceramic tile, marble, and fiberglass. But beware! The circular saw is probably the most dangerous power tool used in the home or the shop.

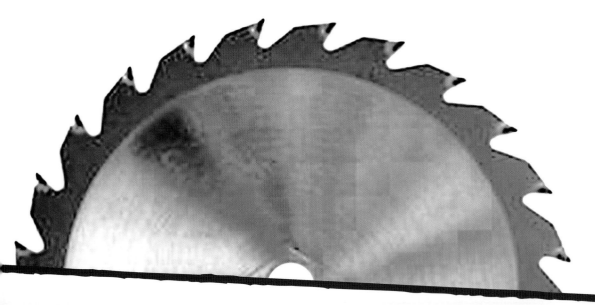

Look for a model with a safety brake that stops the blade from spinning as you release the trigger. Although the blade guard is supposed to snap down and cover the blade quickly, accidents can happen. So, remember that "cutting up" and cutting with a circular saw are two different things that should never be done together. You should always wear safety goggles (or a face shield). And if you're a thrill seeker who loves running with scissors, playing in traffic, and juggling firecrackers, you should also wear a safety helmet and handcuffs.

YOU'RE ONLY AS SHARP AS YOUR BLADE

These tips will help you master any blade work:

TIP Don't use a dull or damaged saw blade, which can actually hurt *you* and not just the wood you're trying to cut. It's worth getting carbide-tipped blades sharpened, but standard steel blades are cheap enough to simply replace when they get dull.

TIP When you start getting into specialized wood-cutting blades, there are two basic types that serve two functions: The first type, which has fewer teeth spaced farther apart, is used to make fast, long rip cuts (with the grain). The second type is used for crosscutting (against the grain) and has more teeth for finer, smoother cuts.

TIP Using a clamped-on straightedge guide with a circular saw, a jigsaw, or even a router makes a precision straight cut.

TIP The limited cutting depth of a circular saw doesn't have to limit you to cutting only thin boards. If you want to cut something thicker, mark your cutting line on the front and back of the piece. After you cut the front, flip over the piece and complete the cut from the back. Still not all the way through? Make cuts on the sides as well. And if you're dealing with something really hefty, get through the middle with your trusty handsaw.

3. COMPOUND MITER SAW

The compound miter saw is an awesome angle-cutting circular saw that is hinged to a small base. It lets you make clean, precision crosscuts at angles up to 45 degrees (on some, 50 degrees), with stops for the most commonly used angles. It's great for cutting trim and 2-by-4s, and is usually the tool of choice of the finish carpenter. With a compound miter saw, you can also tilt the blade at an angle of up to 45 degrees off vertical for bevel cuts. This type of saw is great for notching 2-by-4s by setting the blade depth and not cutting all the way through.

TIP Make sure a miter saw is adjusted properly by using a speed square to align the blade. Loosen the blade's swing arm with a wrench, then press the blade flush against the vertical edge at a 90-degree angle to make perfect square cuts.

TIP If you'll be cutting several pieces to the same (short) length, set up a cutting "stop" by clamping a small piece of 2-by-4 to the fence of the saw. By making just one measurement, you can now do repeated matching cuts.

4. ORBITAL SANDER

This woodworking wizard makes sanding a breeze. The sanding pad rotates in small circles at thousands of revolutions per minute. It's used primarily for finishing work, rather than for rough removal of stock (a belt sander takes more off). It is meant to be used for the final smoothing of wood furniture in preparation for the application of a finish, or between coats of finish. It can also be used to sand rough paint on exterior siding (and between jobs to shape surfboards). Use both hands to guide the sander, but let it do the work — don't apply a lot of pressure. Turn the sander at an angle to go a little deeper, but be gentle — it can leave blemishes.

TIP If your sanding is creating a dust-storm effect in your shop, use a shop vacuum with a hose hooked to the sander — that is, if your model has an exhaust opening that permits.

5. TABLE SAW

Having one big table saw in the shop or a portable bench-top model on the road lets you make accurate cuts in all your board-feet of wood. It's a great tool for cutting large panels or ripping long boards without having to run a marathon with a circular saw and a straightedge.

6. RECIPROCATING SAW

Demolition derby, here I come! Who ever thought tearing stuff down could be so much fun? This tool works like a heavy-duty carving knife to make holes in walls or roofs for new windows, doors, or skylights. It will let you reach hard-to-access places under, in between, and behind. It is also quite versatile — it cuts all kinds of materials. With a quick change to a metal blade, a recip saw can zip through even plumbing pipes and nails.

7. JIGSAW

The blade on this portable saw, also known as a saber saw, goes up and down, letting you get "jiggy" with straight and — most important — intricate curved cuts. Clamp on an edge guide to guarantee a straight cut. A variable-speed model is great for getting the right cutting speed for different materials. The saw tends to shimmy, so push down at the same time as you push forward. The blade can be angled, and you can also carefully plunge it into material (or drill a starting hole) to make a cutout from the middle. Specialty blades add to the range of this saw, letting you cut metal, plastic, or ceramic tile.

8. ELECTRIC PLANER

A hand-held planer is a great tool for shaving down a wooden edge, such as on windows or doors that are sticking in their frames, or to shorten the bottom of a door after installing carpeting. You can also use it to beautify old, weathered wood; it will take off the rough top layer and expose the beautiful grain beneath — of course, you could sand for days instead.

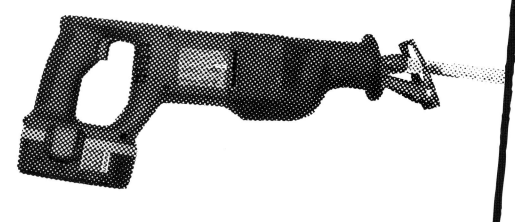

9. FINISH NAILER

This tool is basically a rapid-fire nail gun, which saves huge amounts of time while leaving only tiny nail holes in the wood instead of the "meat tenderizer" look caused by hammering nails. It can be rented or purchased with an additional air compressor and hose, which allows you to have constant power with adjustable pressure. Alternatively, you can use (as I did for the entire first season on *Trading Spaces*) a very portable battery-operated finish or framing nailer, which uses cartridges of carbon dioxide for non-regulated pressure. Electric, corded models are also available.

10. BELT SANDER

When a planer is too much and an orbital sander isn't enough, go with a belt sander, which will remove a fair amount of material at each pass while still allowing a lot of control. This tool is great for leveling off uneven joints where two pieces of wood meet, such as with flooring boards; sanding out flaws or gouges from wood surfaces; trimming some wood off door edges to make them fit better; and rounding edges, such as on a stair tread.

TIP Safety reminder: Wear safety goggles when working with any of these power tools.

TY'S tips

A belt sander can also be turned over and clamped to a table for sanding small pieces of wood held by hand.

TOOLS WITHOUT COMMITMENT

Having a Can-Do-It kit available for small jobs is an absolute home-repair necessity. Keeping a few choice power tools around in the garage lets you become a part-time professional (Overachiever-Beaver). It also allows you to keep your relationships with friends and neighbors alive instead of living on "borrowed" time. But certain specialty power tools that are needed only for "special" jobs can be rented by the hour or the day. For example, a floor nailer, a power washer, a plumbing auger (snake), and a diamond-bladed tile saw all are tools you need only occasionally — not to mention equipment such as long ladders and scaffolding.

TIP Many tool rental places are closed Sundays, so check if their policy allows you to rent a tool on a Saturday and return it first thing Monday morning without being charged for an extra day.

If you borrow tools, there are some rules you should follow:

1. **Buy and use your own "consumables" that go along with the tool, such as blades, drill bits, sanding belts, etc.**

2. **Don't get in over your head by borrowing a tool beyond your skill level. This can leave the owner feeling responsible for any "accident" that might happen. Don't be too proud to ask for safe operating instructions if you're at all uncertain.**

3. **Return the tool as soon as you're done with it. Give the tool back in the same shape it was in when you borrowed it; if something got bent or broken, get it fixed.**

4. **Find ways to show your appreciation. Lend tools in return, or lend a hand when the lender needs help.**

Trust me, you don't find too many skillionaires who lend tools to friends — they almost never come back in the same condition. I don't mind sharing tips and tricks, but it's *my* time, not *our* time, that I waste fixing and realigning my tools after "sharing" them. *If you only knew what I have to go through.*

SAFE-TY FIRST SMART TIPS

DON'T BE STUPID — IT'S NOT SMART

Nothing seems to be safe these days. There are warning labels on coffee cups, CDs, potato chips, even underarm deodorant. It's a good idea to be aware of certain dangers, but I think we may be getting a little carried away. Trust me, I'm sure I should have been wearing a helmet my entire childhood *even when I was inside the house.* Seriously, it's amazing I've made it this far, not to mention becoming a carpenter and working on 40-foot ladders trying to cut plywood one-handed with a circular saw. After seeing a few nasty accidents happen on job sites and having a few close calls of my own, I finally figured out a few things about safety. For example: It's not smart to work alone hanging off the edge of a four-story building with a garden hose tied around a chimney as your "life"-line. *Reaching the soffit wasn't nearly as difficult as reaching for and dialing my cell phone while holding onto the garden hose.* It's safe to say I learned a few lessons that day. The most important was "Don't be stupid."

Also, "If you can't reach it with a ladder rested firmly on level ground, then don't." Because I am an accident and seem to be waiting to happen, I offer some tips for working safely and resisting the urge to act like a total idiot.

- Wear safety goggles when you're using a power tool. Add ear plugs for loud tools such as planers or hammer drills, and a dust mask when working with anything that kicks up dust.

- Before starting a job, make sure you know what you want to do, and what steps you are going to carry out to get there.

- Only work when you're well rested, unhurried, centered, and — if possible today — calm and unstressed. Relax, breathe, and focus mentally on the task. This slows you to a good working pace and makes the job a lot more fun.

- Wear shoes. Being stupid is not being stylish.

TY'S tips

Ask a buddy to help with jobs that require another set of hands. Too long, heavy, or unstable? Don't try to do it all on your own.

TIP Don't leave things lying around. Slobs in this field are a dying breed — or at least hospitalized. Sharp tools on the ground and nails sticking out of boards are the worst kind of cutting-edge technology. (Trust me, they smart.)

TIP Don't overextend your reach or lean to the side on a ladder.

TIP Be bright; don't work in the dark. Keep a work light handy.

TIP Read the labels. Be aware of the dangers of any chemicals you are working with and protect yourself accordingly.

"It is easier to walk through a doorway than to run into a wall."

Tao of Ty

chapter 5
WALLS

GIVE YOUR WALLS A MAKEOVER

Getting plastered isn't all it's cracked up to be. I get a headache just thinking about it. It's much more "trowel" and error than "funnel" and games. It's messy and time-consuming. Unless you're a mud-slinging hotshot, the results can be pretty bumpy. I thank our Maker for *drywall*. It may be more prone than plaster to dents, but it enjoys a few traits that make it a whole lot more fun to hang with. It's a breeze to install, and it's not expensive. The biggest drag about drywall is that the sheets are heavy and awkward to handle. Time to call in favors from your buddies — this will be a true test of your friendship.

Over time, walls — like anything else — get old, become sick, and suffer the occasional injury. A house can settle on its foundation, leaving cracks. Water infiltration will make plaster crumble. And if you hang with people who have an anger-management problem, fist-sized dents may suddenly appear. These are problems no ointment can cure. And while some like to ascribe "character" to these scars, most homeowners prefer to have nice, healthy, boring walls that are smooth and blemish-free.

So, prepare yourself, and now, if you're ready to get wild and crazy and plastered, here is my own personal *twelve-step program.*

1. **Accept that you have a problem.**
   Assess the damage.

2. **Put the past behind you.**
   Get rid of your pain in the lath.

3. **Be prepared.**
   Have the right tools and materials on hand.

4. **Overcome obstacles.**
   Remove moldings, cover plates, and anything else in the way.

5. **Get help.**
   You'll need it.

6. **Find support**.
   Mark your studs.

7. **Installation.**
   New rules and measures.

8. **Know the drill.**
   Screwing drywall.

9. **Stick to cleaner joints.**
   Taping seams.

10. **Don't get stuck in the mud.**
    Consistency is important.

11. **Stay dust-free by sponging your joints**.
    Finish your joints.

12. **Celebrate.**
    Sheet, man, you rock!

1 ACCEPT THAT YOU HAVE A PROBLEM

ASSESS THE DAMAGE

You might not hear them, but your walls could be silently screaming for help. After years spent hanging onto a plastered, "broken" home, suffering from neglect or abandonment, the walls around you could be showing signs of a long, abused life. These "age lines," consisting of cracks, holes, and scars in the walls' plastered face, can be hidden by a "cover-up" patch, or a complete "makeover" or "facelift" can be done by installing new drywall over the old plaster. If what ails your walls is caused by moisture, you'd better figure out where the water is coming from and solve this problem first.

2 PUT THE PAST BEHIND YOU

GET RID OF YOUR PAIN IN THE LATH

If your house was built before the '50s, odds are its walls are made of plaster. Back before drywall days, highly skilled plasterers worked their magic, applying several layers of plaster over wooden strips called lath that were attached to the studs. If you decide to keep the original old walls, but you feel that the giant cracks and holes in them give your home a little *too* much character, you can patch the plaster, reviving it to look pretty close to the original. On the other hand, if you're ready for a fresh, clean look, you could choose to cover the entire old plaster wall with new drywall, hung right on top of it. Forget about major re-plastering yourself; call in the hired guns for that.

You can repair small, shallow dings or cracks in plaster (after cleaning out loose bits) with joint compound or plaster of Paris. For very small repairs, such as nail holes, you can use spackling compound. For huge holes — don't freak out — things have to get worse before they get better. Enlarge the hole, using a cold chisel to remove damaged plaster on each side of the hole until you reach the halfway point on the studs. If the lath is so badly damaged that you need to cut it away, do so carefully with a keyhole saw or a jigsaw. The more you disturb the lath, the greater your risk of getting brained by chunks of falling plaster.

Draw and cut the opening into a rectangle. Cut a matching patch of drywall, making it a tiny bit smaller, then screw the patch to the studs and apply joint compound to bring everything up to the surface of the surrounding wall.

Joint compound is available premixed in tubs and buckets or as a powder that must be mixed with water in a bucket. It is best to prep the joint compound using a mixing bit attached to a drill, much like a cake mixer whipping batter. Dampen the repaired area before applying the joint compound.

APPLICATION: Slap on the joint compound with a flat plasterer's trowel, skimming back and forth. Apply several thin coats, feathering out the edges so there will be less to sand. Let the patch dry between coats. Try to match the texture of the existing wall by "stippling" the surface of the patch with something like a scrub brush or sponge — be creative. Let the patch dry and *voilà*.

TIP Get the drywall patch as close to the surface as possible by using thicker-than-standard drywall or nailing furring strips to the studs. The top and bottom furring strips also provide a screwing surface for the upper and lower edges of the patch.

3 BE PREPARED

HAVE THE RIGHT TOOLS AND MATERIALS ON HAND

I'll never be accused of being your classic Boy Scout, but to me, "Be prepared" is a bang-on motto for home repair — maybe some other things, too? Before you begin a job, pull together the tools and materials you need so your work will progress smoothly, without the constant interruption of having to run back to the store for something.

You'll need to get in drywall, today's wall covering of choice. Also known as wallboard or by trade names such as Sheetrock™, drywall is made of gypsum encased in paper. It comes in panels in a variety of thicknesses and sizes, and is easy to work with. It ranges from 1/4 inch to 5/8 inch thick, and while the 1/2-inch sheets are the most common, go thicker if you want more strength and better soundproofing qualities, or if your studs are more than 16 inches apart. The typical sheet is 4-by-8 feet, but you can also get lengths of up to 16 feet. You'll need drywall screws, and cutting tools include a utility knife and drywall saw. To finish the seams, get joint tape, joint compound, a mixing bit, a mud pan, a few different sizes of drywall knives, drywall sandpaper, and a drywall sponge or sanding block. For repairs, add spackling compound and a plasterer's trowel to your shopping cart.

4 OVERCOME OBSTACLES

REMOVE MOLDINGS, COVER PLATES, AND ANYTHING ELSE IN THE WAY

Now it's time to strip everything off the walls you're about to work on. Take off any trim: shoe moldings, baseboards, crown molding, and door and window trim. Careful! You may want to re-use these pieces afterward. Unscrew electrical cover plates, thermostats, wall-mounted phones, and the like. Keep in mind that if you're putting up drywall directly over plaster, the electrical boxes will have to be extended to bring them out flush with the new surface. *A professional electrician should extend the electrical boxes.*

YOU'LL NEED IT

Oh, the joyous memories of endless runs to the home improvement store, loading a cart with drywall. It's usually packaged in sheets of two, and man, is it heavy. If you think you can lift two 4-by-8 sheets by yourself, dream on, Superman! What I suggest is that you take someone with you, buy him lunch, and then take him to your place to help you drag the sheets inside. Maybe you can even persuade him to stick around to help you with the installation.

Now, once you've brought the drywall inside, crank up the jams and get cracking. Well, actually, we're jumping ahead of ourselves. First things first:

TIP There is less work in cutting than in taping. When buying drywall, simplify your life by getting the exact size sheets — or longer. For vertical installation, if your wall height is more than 8 feet, buy longer sheets. This will save you from having to finish so many seams.

TIP If you're installing drywall on a newly framed wall, with the studs exposed, start at the center. But before you hang any sheets, pencil stud location marks on the floor and ceiling so you'll know where your studs are once the drywall goes up. Now, you're ready to go.

TY'S tips

When buying drywall, take a buddy with you, buy him lunch, and take him home to help you drag the sheets inside. See if you can persuade him to stick around to help you with the installation. Offer beer.

6 FIND SUPPORT

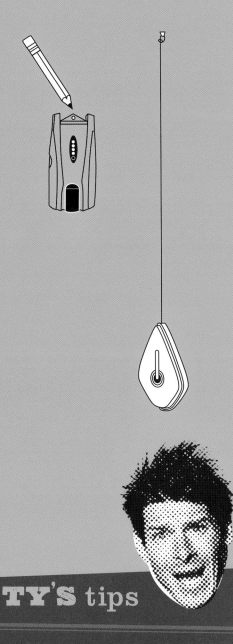

MARK YOUR STUDS

First, you need to find yourself a few studs — you could probably use their help! Mark the locations, then make sure you don't cover up the marks, or you'll be trying to guess where all the studs are when it comes time to screw.

If you're hanging drywall on top of an old plaster wall, find each stud using a stud finder and mark the location. Then, with a 6-foot level, extend the marks onto the ceiling and the floor with a pencil. By doing this, your marks will still be visible when the drywall sheet is in place and the studs are hidden behind it. If you have removed all the old plaster and lath, or if you're working on a newly-built wall, the studs will be exposed and you can simply mark the locations on the ceiling and floor.

Once a drywall sheet is tacked up with a few screws, use a chalk line to snap a line from the mark on the ceiling to the mark on the floor, leaving a "stud line" on the drywall. If you don't have a chalk line, draw a stud line with a 6-foot level and a pencil, using your centered marks on the floor and ceiling as a guide. Now, take aim at those stud lines and finish the screwing.

A stud finder, by the way, isn't a dating service — it's a battery-operated tool that signals when it detects solid wood under it. Once you find one stud, the others are usually spaced 16 inches apart on center (measured from the middle of each stud), but can be spaced up to 24 inches apart. A stud finder is not foolproof; it may not sense deep enough or may give a false reading. *And there is nothing quite like the frustration of thinking you've found a good strong stud, only to be disappointed when the stud turns out to be a weak pain in the lath.*

TY'S tips

If you can't find a stud with a stud finder (or a dating service), try using the old "knock-knock" technique. Go along the wall knocking with your knuckles, listening for a different, more "solid" sound. Then, using a 1/16-inch drill bit, drill repeatedly at this location until you find wood in the bit.

INSTALLATION

NEW RULES AND MEASURES

Before installing your first sheet of drywall, you'll have to eyeball the area to determine if any cuts will have to be made in the sheet before it goes up — such as around openings at windows or doors, or at electrical boxes. You may be able to save yourself some work here. If you can measure out a 4-foot-wide stretch of studs that don't need cutouts between them, install your first sheet here. But chances are, there will be no way of getting around having to make cutouts. So, beginning at a corner, measure horizontally over to the first cutout location, then measure down from the ceiling. Transfer these measurements to your drywall sheet and make the cut with a drywall saw. And what do you do now that your drywall is cut? I'd say cut loose, at least for a few minutes, to psych yourself up for screwing the drywall into place.

To make a straight cut (edge to edge) in drywall, snap a chalk line on the front of the sheet to mark your cut. Using a straightedge, score this line a few times with a utility knife, going 1/8 inch to 1/4 inch deep. Make a final pass without the guide, then snap the panel along the line and slice the back paper. To cut out a notch from a corner, use a drywall saw for one edge, then score and snap the other edge as for a straight cut. He shoots, he scores!

TIP Know your front from your back. Drywall's front side, which is the side to be painted, is tapered along the long edges. The back side isn't meant to be painted.

TIP If you'll be making a lot of straight cuts in drywall, get a drywall T-square. You place the guide of this 4-foot-long straight-edge along the edge of the drywall sheet for a guaranteed perpendicular line.

NOTCHING AND PATCHING

There are people out there who are dangerous for walls. I call these people, among other things, door slammers. You know the type, usually the drama queens with a thirst for attention, notorious for climaxing a temper tantrum by putting a fist through a wall or slamming the door so hard it bounces back out of the frame, burying the doorknob into perfectly painted drywall. Nice. A charming bunch, those door slammers, but hey, at least there's never a dull moment. Frankly, though, I can live without that type of excitement.

Well, in the event that your walls are hit-and-run victims of a door slammer or a hole puncher, you will need to do some patching. The good news is that with drywall, patching is pretty easy. For a small hole (up to 1/2 inch), you can use fast-drying spackling compound. For a big hole, if it is round or has uneven edges, start by making it as square as possible: Use a level and draw a rectangle or square on the wall, then cut along the marks with a utility knife or drywall saw. You can cut back to the midpoint on adjacent studs in order to provide a surface to screw in the patch. Or, if the hole is isolated between studs, use two 2-by-4 braces 3 to 4 inches longer than the opening. Insert each brace into the hole and get a friend to hold it tight against the back of the drywall. Screw through the drywall into each end of the brace. Now, when you put the patch into the hole, it will have something solid to support it, preventing it from being pushed all the way through and falling into the space behind the wall. Forever.

Next, cut a new piece of drywall a tiny bit smaller than the hole getting patched. When placing the patch, don't push too hard; cover it with a flat piece of wood and gently tap around the area. Screw the patch into place, then tape the joints with mesh tape and apply joint compound.

facelifts for walls

THINGS YOU MAY NEED

Drywall sheet(s)	Drywall knives
Joint tape (mesh is best)	Drywall sandpaper
Joint compound (mud)	Drywall sponge
Mud pan	(or sanding block)
Drill with mixing bit and	Sponges
screw gun	Respirator or dust mask
Bucket (5-gallon)	Safety goggles

8 KNOW THE DRILL

SCREWING DRYWALL

Once the drywall sheet is cut and/or notched, make sure it fits. Place the sheet against the wall and check that it sits plumb with the studs. If necessary, fit a shim under the bottom edge on one side to line it up with the studs. Leave space to fasten the adjacent sheet to the same stud; the two sheets have to make a tight fit at the seam. You'll find screwing easier if you aren't trying to hold the sheet in place at the same time, so start by securing it with a couple of screws at the top and sides. Use 1 1/4-inch or 1 1/2-inch drywall screws (2-inch if you're going in over a plaster wall), spacing them 12 inches apart along the marked studs. At the joints, toenail the screws (drive them in at an angle) and stagger them vertically in relation to the screws on the adjacent sheet. Keep going this way, installing the drywall sheet by sheet.

TIP By spending a few bucks on a square-drive bit for your drill, you can use square-drive screws. These screws are better than the typical Phillips-head type in that they don't strip out as easily.

9 STICK TO CLEANER JOINTS

TAPING SEAMS

Joint compound, aka mud, can be bought premixed in various sizes of tubs and buckets or unmixed in bags. If you go with the unmixed type, prepare it in a bucket by adding water and using a mixing bit installed in your drill.

Taping the joints: After you have hung all the drywall, your body will probably feel like that of an injured quarterback who has been sacked back to back and is now heading off the field to get a few swollen joints taped. So, break out the Ben-Gay™ because now it's time to tape the drywall joints.

There are two different tapes to choose from: paper or mesh. Paper is cheaper, but mesh is easier because it has adhesive backing to help it stick to the wall. This means you can sometimes tape off the entire room before you even start slinging mud. Mesh is also stronger for repairs. Paper tape requires skimming the joint first with mud, giving the paper something to stick to, then applying another thicker coat to hide the tape.

TIP To apply the first coat of mud, start at the top and drag a 4- or 6-inch drywall knife down, then stroke up from the bottom until the strips of mud meet in the middle. Ease up on the pressure and gently lift away. Don't worry too much if the mud isn't perfectly smooth — it's only the first coat. Let the mud dry a full day before you sand or sponge, then apply another coat with a 10-inch knife, feathering out the edges even further. The final "skim" coat is a very thin layer, applied to ensure a smooth finish. Add more water to the mud and mix it again every time you use it. Stay wet and loose, baby! Stick and move!

10 DON'T GET STUCK IN THE MUD

CONSISTENCY IS IMPORTANT

When applying joint compound, regardless of whether you are using premixed or the type you mix yourself, make sure you have the right consistency. Even the premixed needs to be mixed again, and you can do this by adding a touch of water and mixing using a mixer bit that fits into your drill. Keep mixing until the mud looks like cake icing, but please, even if it looks tasty, *don't eat it.* (I've tried it and it sucks — after all, it is mud.) Now, it is important to keep the joint compound smooth and clean, which means don't reuse old mud, which can be full of dry chunks, cat hair, popcorn, and other unmentionables.

TIP To cover screwheads, swipe on mud with a vertical motion and remove the excess with a horizontal motion. Two coats of mud are usually plenty for these babies.

TIP One way to *keep it clean* is to have a bucket on hand to discard dirty joint compound — instead of putting it back into your mud pan. Mud pans come in plastic or shiny aluminum (which can double as stylish planters). Both types have a metal edge that you use to scrape clean the blade of your drywall knife. Both your pan and knives can get rusty, so clean and dry them after each use.

TIP For a quicker fix, use fast-drying joint compound. But only mix a small amount at a time, making it a little wetter than you would regular joint compound to keep it from drying before it is applied to the wall.

TIP It's going to get a little humid, so have fun — get naked (kidding?) and if it makes your friend or helper uncomfortable, wear a tool belt. *But don't forget the deodorant* because the room is going to need a stick-up.

TY'S tips

Quick fix for nail or screw holes, or small patches: Use spackling compound; it dries faster than mud.

11 STAY DUST-FREE BY SPONGING YOUR JOINTS

FINISH YOUR JOINTS

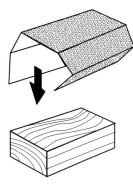

Now that you have taped your aching joints and rubbed on Ben-Gay™, better lather up with lotion because it's about to get dusty. It isn't called drywall for nothing. Okay, there's no way to sugarcoat this: If you plan on sanding the joints with sandpaper, everything in the vicinity — and beyond — is about to be covered in dust. Here are some tips on keeping dust storms to a minimum.

WHEN YOU SAND:

TIP Buy lots of plastic drop sheets or trash bags. Place them over your computer, TV, stereo, *everything*. Use painter's tape to seal your doorways in plastic. Lay drop sheets on the floor. This will help. Trust me, I speak the truth.

TIP You can make a sanding block out of a scrap piece of 2-by-4. But the hard edges can leave grooves, so splurge and get sanding sponges or a drywall sanding block. These blocks are faced with a rubber pad for a softer surface, and you can fit a pole on some for high reaching. Sanding by hand is tiring, so keep the Ben-Gay™ handy — not to mention a handkerchief for that special brand of joint compound being prepared inside your nostrils. Do yourself a favor and wear a respirator, or at least a dust mask, and put on safety goggles to keep the dust out of your eyes. As I always say, doing it by hand is cheap, but not necessarily easy.

TIP Starting with medium (100-grit or 120-grit) paper made specifically for drywall, sand mainly the edges using a circular motion. Switch to fine-grade paper (say, 150 grit) and continue until the compound is completely smooth. If your surface is already ridge-free, you can start with 150-grit paper.

TIP Now, there will still be tons of dust on the floors and in the cracks of tongue-and-groove boards. If you have sawdust left over from woodworking projects, add a little water to it to make a wet mulch. Toss the mixture on the dusty floor, then sweep or vacuum it up. The result is amazing. If you don't have any sawdust, take fresh cat litter (only a low-dust, non-clumping type!), wet it, and use it the same way.

SPONGING

The best way to sand joint compound without making a lot of dust is to give up on sanding and take up sponging. I don't mean moving in with friends to couch-surf for six to eight weeks. I mean actually using a wet sponge instead of sandpaper to smooth out the rough edges of the dried joint compound on the joints. This technique is fast, cheap, and completely dust-free, so put away your lotions, pick up a few large, soft sponges and a 5-gallon bucket of water, and follow these steps on smoothing joints with a sponge. Make sure the joint compound is not completely dry when you do this, but dry enough so you don't rub it all off. This can be a little tricky, and works best if your coats of mud are thin and even.

1. Using a wet sponge, wipe in circular motions, concentrating on the outer edges of the joints. What you want to do is smooth the rough outer edges without removing too much joint compound from the middle and exposing the joint tape underneath.

    TIP: Keep your sponge and water clean by rinsing the sponge frequently and changing the water before it gets too dirty.

2. On the second pass, sponge quickly with a wetter sponge. Let the seam dry again and come back with a drier sponge for the finish smoothing. You may still need to sand a bit at this point.

3. Prepare to paint — and you thought you were done.

Sponging is a great way to smooth over mud joints while staying dust-free. Just ask any sponge — he (or she) will tell you that anything free is sure worth looking into. Now that you have been spared a lot of sanding and your walls are sponged smooth, you're ready to prime and paint. The prep work is over.

SEAL THOSE GAPS

CAULK (THE INS AND OUTS)

I paid my way through art school by working as a carpenter by day and being a student by night. I was one of many on a crew of framers and finishers. Framers build the frame of a house, and finishers install all the interior trim and molding. The so-called "delicate" work of finishers requires precise measurements with angled cuts to ensure tight fits. There was, however, one finisher on my team who was notorious for cutting boards too short. I think his name *was* Shorty. Anyway, Shorty would cut the molding, then hand it to me to be nailed in place. Upon close inspection, I would announce, "That last one is 1/2 inch off." Shorty would snap back, "Caulk it."

Well, needless to say, caulk has more uses than hiding mistakes. Unlike Shorty, it fills in the gaps, is quite flexible, is available in a range of colors, and can make your home nice and warm. It can also save you money by keeping the desirable temperature in, and the undesirable temperature out.

WHY CAULK?

Whenever there is fluctuation in temperature or humidity, gaps and cracks can open up in the outer shell of a house. This is because different construction materials swell and shrink to different extents. Do a tour of your house, looking for any openings to the outside (especially where two unlike materials touch), and caulk them. Indoors, around sinks and tubs, caulk will keep water from getting in where it shouldn't. Even if the materials move a bit, caulk is flexible and will hang in there to do the job. Be sure to use a product that is appropriate for both the material and and the location.

TIP: If you plan on painting the caulk you apply, make sure the label specifies that it can be painted. If you're painting before the caulk is fully cured, run your brush over it very lightly.

WHERE TO PUT YOUR CAULK

Caulk can seal joints anywhere there is an opening in the outer skin of the house or where two perpendicular surfaces meet: wall corners, door and window frames, dryer vents and exhaust fans, plumbing and electrical entry points, along the top of the foundation wall, around air conditioners, and up on the roof at the base of the chimney and at vents. Wherever possible, caulk both the inside and outside of the opening.

In kitchens, bathrooms, and laundry rooms, caulk any seams that should be watertight, such as between a sink and the countertop, and between a tub and the wall and floor.

TYPES OF CAULK

Acrylic latex — interior/exterior: door and window frames, drywall, moldings, plumbing fixtures.

Siliconized acrylic latex — interior/exterior: same applications as acrylic latex, but silicone additive gives improved adhesion and flexibility.

Silicone — interior; waterproof: sinks and tubs, ceramic tiles, glass, metal, plumbing fixtures.

Thermoplastic — exterior; highly elastic: doors and windows, siding, gutters, masonry, plastic boards.

Butyl (synthetic rubber) — exterior: masonry, metal, wood.

Masonry (polyurethane) — floors, walls, sidewalks.

Roof (bituminous pitch) — shingles, flashing, foundation walls.

What is caulk? Caulk, or caulking, is a flexible sealant that goes on wet and hardens as it cures. It is usually sold in tubes and used in a gun that squeezes the caulking out of the tube's plastic tip.

The one thing that you can always expect when you work with caulk is that you are going to get a little goo on your hands. One thing leads to another, and before you know it, your gun is spewing goo uncontrollably from the tip. The trick to mastering an out-of-control caulking gun is to keep your thumb on the pressure-release lever and have a rag on hand to clean up the mess with ease. Even more important, be sure that you are using the right caulk for the job. Although caulks may all look the same, there are different ones made for different jobs; some may be labeled as sealants. Depending on the caulk in question, getting it off may require more than soap and water. Read the label to see what the manufacturer recommends to dissolve it.

HOW TO USE YOUR CAULK

Well, if it seems pretty easy, it is. You put your caulk in a crack or joint and you give your gun a squeeze. But don't get overexcited. The more caulk you use, the bigger the mess you'll make. It's best to take your time.

Step 1: Prepare the crack: Make sure the crack is free of debris, brushing or blowing it out (wear safety goggles!) or using a putty knife to remove it. If the crack is more than 1/2 inch deep, stuff in foam backer rod or other filler to build up a base before caulking.

Step 2: Load your caulking gun and use a utility knife to make a diagonal cut through the end of the nozzle on the caulk tube. Insert a long nail or piece of stiff wire into the nozzle to break the seal.

Step 3: Place the nozzle of your gun at the top of the crack. Holding the gun at an angle, press the trigger. Slide the nozzle along the crack at a constant speed to lay a nice, uniform bead of caulk in the opening. Let go of the trigger while there is still a bit of the crack to be filled and hit the pressure-release lever — the caulk doesn't stop flowing right away.

Step 4: If you want, you can flatten out the bead of caulk or set it into the crack a bit more: For water-based caulk, run a wet finger along it; otherwise, use a cloth dipped in the appropriate solvent.

Step 5: Smoke 'em if you've got 'em. That was awesome.

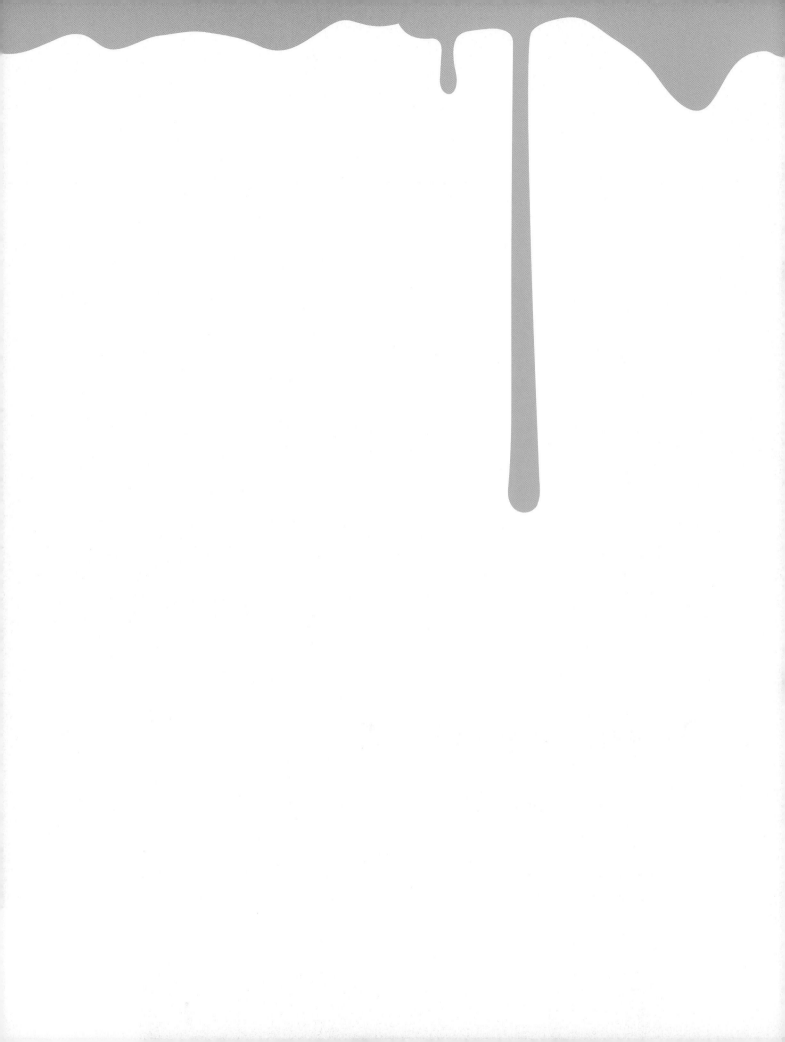

"I want to know one thing. What is color?"

6

chapter

A PICTURE PAINTS
A THOUSAND WORDS

PAINTING

You'll already know from watching episodes of *Trading Spaces* that paint is the first miracle worker of every successful renovation. Even if you aren't up to doing much more, painting a room can lift it from ordinary to extraordinary in a few hours — and without breaking the bank. What more could you ask? A mere one-gallon paint can for a whole new look? Just do it! But hold on. Painting is more than just covering the walls; it expresses your style. (It also protects your home, but let's just deal with the inspiration.) Your walls are a canvas and *you*, my friend, are holding the brush.

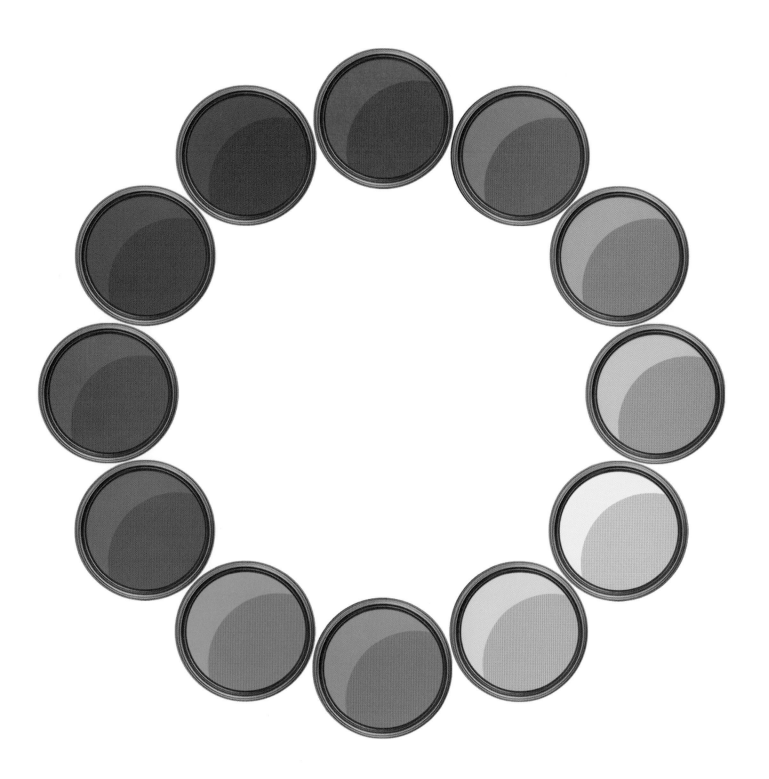

Blank canvases need a little preparation, though. I'm sure that after all the drywall installation, sanding, and dust inhalation, you're probably about ready for a little rest and relaxation. But don't stop now. You're ahead of the game, and the good news is that you've already done most of the preparation.

Before you slap on color, you've got to prime the walls, not only to protect from wear and tear, but also to save on paint — at about $20 a gallon, it's a bargain, but not if you need several coats because you skipped the priming.

EASY

old paint

A good latex drywall primer is best for several reasons: It *seals* the drywall much better than regular paint and takes only one, maybe two, really good coats. If the walls are stained with anything as bad as rust, mildew, or ink, it's better to use an oil-based primer (such as Kilz™), but then you should be sure to wear a respirator.

TIP Got some old paint hanging around that might just come in handy? A quick, fashionable way to get rid of the lumps in it is to use a pair of panty hose — honest! Just grab an old pair you've got stored next to your jockstrap in your sock drawer, and stretch the crotch or a foot of the hose over the top of a 5-gallon bucket. You might need to use clamps to hold the hose in place. Now, pour the old paint slowly into the bucket through the filter. Watch out for "runs" in the hose (a filtering faux pas!).

TY'S ADVICE

Repairing Paint Jobs at a Later Date

Whether you had your paint mixed at the store or you mixed your own color from leftover odds and ends, whatever is left over will probably end up getting stuck on a storage shelf. Unlike wine, paint does not get better with age. But you don't have to throw it out just because it is dried up, cracked, or full of boogers — what I call the chunks of goo that grow inside cans of old paint.

Color matching is not an exact science, so it makes sense to save leftover paint for touch-ups. You can use it time and again for repairs, as long as it is filtered each time.

CHEAP

A more affordable alternative is to prime your drywall with discounted or salvaged and filtered paint. Make sure the paint is a latex interior with a *flat* finish. You can often find miscolored paint on sale in 1-gallon, or sometimes 5-gallon, containers. You might even get lucky and find a color similar to the one you've chosen to paint your walls.

TIP If you really want to save some cash, find several gallons of paint with the same sheen (flat), but not necessarily the same color, and mix them in a 5-gallon bucket. We call this *boxing* the paint, and it should always be done with the same kind of paint. This is a way to create a color from several others. If you have to paint a lot of walls the same color, boxing the paint means that all the paint is exactly the same color mix. (The name boxing comes from the fact that gallons usually come in a box of four.)

Boxing paint is always a good idea. This way, if you ever need to touch up a larger area of a room, you will have plenty of the exact formula ready for a perfect color match, without having to repaint the entire room.

discounted paint

CHOOSING COLORS

You don't invite people who get on your nerves to stay in your home, do you? If you're normal — like me! — you're looking for harmony in your nest, so keep that in mind when choosing your colors. The emotions, moods, and personality that colors bring will surround you every day. Be sure you like them well enough before you commit to a long-term relationship.

If you need help deciding, choose your favorite from the six color swatches to the right. Just go with your instinct. Then, turn the page and read the text on your color to see if it matches your personality. Okay, go for it!

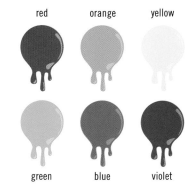

red   orange   yellow

green   blue   violet

Red

Red sure gets your attention all right! It packs an emotional wallop and symbolizes love, rage, courage, and passion. Those who choose red are active and aggressive go-getters. They may be impulsive, and are constantly striving and looking for all the thrills that life has to offer.

Violet

Aha! Now we know the real you. The choice of this regal and luxurious color tells us you are a sensual and passionate beast. If you like violets and purples, you are probably one-of-a-kind, oh so sensitive, and obviously observant. Betcha you love surprises and anything unusual, and you're likely creative and artistically talented. A complex personality? I think so!

Orange

Pumpkins, autumn leaves, spices . . . . In its brightest tones orange is lively, cheerful, and invigorating. When it's darkened to burnt tones, orange can be exotic. If orange is your choice, you probably have lots of energy, and you like to be social. Family and friends find you agreeable and fun to be with. You are creative, but you aren't a flake. You like a bit of structure in your life.

Blue

Tranquil, cooling, soothing blue. It speaks of comfort and serenity. If you chose blue, you have a basic need for a calm, stress-free existence. You're loyal, conservative, and sensitive to others. You're calm, cool, and collected — in other words, totally cool.

Green

The color of all nature's living things, green represents freshness, harmony, and peacefulness. Green symbolizes the intense, but quiet power of nature. If you chose green, you like your space to be calm, balanced, restful. You're affectionate, secure, and — like all growing things — good to have on the face of Earth.

Yellow

Remember the old yellow Smiley Face? It was yellow because this is the color of joy. Yellow is the happiest of all colors, and radiates enlightenment, sunlight, and spirituality. If your favorite color is yellow, you're probably smart, imaginative, and communicative. You look forward to the future. In other words, you're a cockeyed optimist.

Don't worry if the description isn't right on. Keep in mind that each color has many different tints and shades that cover an even wider range of personalities and moods. For example, if you chose red but don't think of yourself as aggressive, remember that the reds go all the way from baby-girl pink to manly deep burgundy. Somewhere between the two, you'll find a shade or tint that matches the inner you. Finding powerful color combinations from the many possibilities is the creative part — and it's fun.

COLOR WHEEL

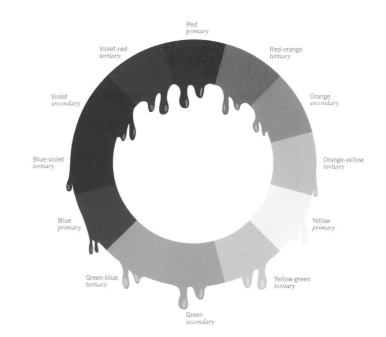

PRIMARY

SECONDARY

TERTIARY

Using the Color Wheel

Using the color wheel is the best way to find color solutions that work well. There are lots of different color schemes to choose from, and you only have to please yourself . . . well, okay, and all the other people you live with. Understanding the color wheel can give you a head start. If you ever took grade school art classes, you probably learned about the color wheel. If you didn't, or if you happened to be fooling around instead of paying attention, here's how it works. The color wheel has all 12 colors of the rainbow in the same sequence, but instead of being in an arc, the colors are brought around to form a circle.

PRIMARY COLORS: Three of the colors are what we call primary: red, blue, and yellow. Red, blue, and yellow can't be formed by mixing any other colors. They just *are*. And they are the base of all other colors, which, it's safe to guess, is why they're called primary.

SECONDARY COLORS: When you mix equal amounts of any two primary colors, you get a secondary color: green, orange, or violet. Red + yellow = orange, blue + yellow = green, and red + blue = violet.

TERTIARY COLORS: These are any mixture of a primary and an adjacent secondary color: orange-red, yellow-orange, yellow-green, blue-green, blue-violet, and red-violet (purple). They are located between the primary and the secondary colors on the color wheel.

When you look at the entire wheel, the colors divide into warm and cool areas. The reds, oranges, and (most) yellows are warm, while the blues, greens, and purples are cool. Of course, you can have many tones of each color simply by adding different amounts of white or black. The colors that lie beside each other have a common pigment and are harmonious, especially those between two primaries. Colors that are directly opposite each other are called complementary and produce the greatest contrast.

So much for the theory. It may seem a little heavy, but it can really help you find solutions. For example, when I was trying to find a color to complement, but not contrast with the puke-green color of my shower, I found out that a primary color can sometimes complement a secondary color and vice versa. I had been having a tough time finding anything that wasn't gross. Finally, I realized that because puke green is a mix of yellow and green, and because green is made from yellow and blue, my answer might be a blue. Sure enough, I found a nice powder blue that worked beautifully as an accent, and left the room looking bright and clean — which is helpful when your shower is puke green and shaped like a bedpan. Complementary colors (remember, they're opposite each other on the wheel) work well together, too, although they produce more of a contrast. You don't necessarily have to change the dominant color of a room; instead, you can simply change the value or shade of one particular accent color. The point is that you have more than one option to make a room work.

Some people want their rooms to match the color of their curtains, artwork, bedspreads — even their pets. I have a friend, Drea, whose mother painted and decorated her condo to match the colors of her Himalayan cat. And I don't mean just the condo she lived in; I mean the entire 12-story building. Choosing colors to match certain objects can work, as long as there is a variance in the chosen colors' tints or values. For example, using a light blue or medium blue to *accent*, not match, a royal blue works. This is called a monochromatic color scheme and is pretty simple to create.

Then, there are people who like to use paint to create a theme. My grandmother painted my boyhood bedroom, which I shared with my brother, in red, white, and blue stripes, complete with matching striped curtains and striped trash cans. It was all very patriotic, but the colored stripes not only competed with each other, but also incited fights to break out between my brother and me because we felt like we were locked up in a prison cell.

A color can have a serious effect on your outlook. Have you ever noticed how schools and other institutions are painted very neutral, "calm" colors? There is a reason for this. Psychologists have found that color changes in people's surroundings can actually lead to behavior changes. *(I know some homeowners on* Trading Spaces *who underwent changes when colors were switched.)* Some studies also show that the darker the color, the darker the mood of the people placed inside the room *(but I'm not at all sure that this will stop Hilda from painting a room black velvet)*.

So remember, when choosing your paint colors, you are choosing the mood you want to create in your living space. If you're going to change the mood in your room, make sure your room doesn't take over and change your whole mindset. I suggest that you give your room what you wish you could give yourself every day, maybe sunlight *(brightness)*, relaxation *(calm)*, or memories of exotic places and tastes *(the colors of your favorite places of travel)*. Think about the ocean, wildflowers, desert sands, blue sky, crisp apples, mountain ferns — colors that remind you of your favorite places and experiences. I chose to use all fruit and vegetable colors in most areas of my house. I mixed them all myself, adding pigment and paint to achieve a variety of different colors, but all have the same neutral shade. My goal was to use each room as an accent color to the next. Standing in the kitchen, you can see the colors gradually change from cantaloupe to mustard to olive — and never be too far from the fridge when the munchies hit after staring at the walls all day.

I wanted to give each room its own flavor and style, one that gives the feeling you're traveling to different exotic places without having to leave the house. I used a variety of green shades: avocado, olive, and sage; and accented them with mustard, cantaloupe, and powder blue. I took bright colors and made them more neutral by adding warm, earthy colors to the paint. For example, I added a golden tan color to a bright lemon yellow to get a rich mustard. This helped keep the colors in the same hue, or value, and kept the colors calm and relaxing. Complementary colors added a touch of spice.

When you're choosing the colors of your next exotic renovation, your destination doesn't always have to be hot and spicy. Chilling out with crisp, cool colors can quench your thirst for a refreshing change of climate. Accenting warm colors with cool colors can be a little tricky. It's best to stay in one climate. But it's your vacation renovation, so why not accent that spicy saffron yellow room with a wall painted spearmint? If you use only one contrasting color as an accent wall, it just might work. Be sure to take plenty of antacid, and, if you will pardon my French, *bon voyage!*

To save money for other materials, I purchased all the paint for my house from a salvage yard. The paint was really cheap because it was originally mixed incorrectly or was left over from a big job. I paid $1 a gallon, or $6 for a 5-gallon container.

I painted most of my kitchen white for two reasons: White can make a room seem bigger as well as brighter. Also, white was the one contrast to all the other rooms, which are painted different citrus colors, and to a cantaloupe orange chair rail that skirted the kitchen. To get that particular shade of cantaloupe, I had to mix a couple of colors together until they evolved into the perfect melon. But even someone with a perfect melon can have trouble choosing colors. There is no perfect way to be certain that a color is right, but there is definitely a way of knowing when it is wrong. The puke-green color of the shower and toilet in the master bath of my home is a really good example of a "wrong" color. Since they are made of fiberglass and porcelain, the color could not be changed. So, I needed to choose a color that would complement and not complicate the color scheme. In addition to being a skilled carpenter, I am also an artist trained in color theory. I do not, however, have a per- fect melon when it comes to finding a color that complements puke green. What many people don't realize about color is that you don't nec- essarily want to match color to color, but instead to accent one color by using another complementary color.

USING A BRUSH: IT'S ALL IN THE WRIST

Once the color has been chosen and mixed, you're ready to paint. But don't go reaching for that roller yet. Grab a brush, baby! And not just any old brush. Choosing the right brush is more important than you think. Brushes are important tools and should be treated as such. At no time should they be left out to dry with paint on them or stuck in a bucket. If you don't believe me, ask Frank. Many of you who watch *Trading Spaces* know my good friend Frank. Frank has more brushes than a hardware store. And he will be the first to tell you: *Take care of your brushes and they will take care of you.*

Like anything else, you get what you pay for, and this is especially true with brushes. I do not recommend that you purchase the "value pack." Quantity rarely equals quality. Instead, buy a brush that fits your hand comfortably. If you are starting out, use a 2-inch or a 3-inch brush. Make sure the brush is made of quality Chinese bristles for oil paint, or nylon bristles for latex paint. A good brush should cost between $12 and $20, but it will last a long time if properly cleaned and stored. Give your brushes the same love and care that you give your other tools.

TIP To keep the paint can from getting too messy, with runs down the side and the like, poke holes in the rim using a nail and hammer. This will allow paint to drip back inside the can.

You're now ready to "cut in." Basically, this means painting a strip around the entire room where the walls meet the ceiling and the floor, and around window frames, door moldings, and other trim. You can use a plastic edging tool or apply good-quality painter's tape so your lines are neat and straight, and so you don't get any paint on the ceilings or trim. One or two brush widths is enough to cut in.

The trick to all painting, brushing or rolling, is to have the right amount of paint on your brush (or roller). Too much and you get the runs (which is never pretty). And without enough paint on your brush (or roller), you usually end up having to add a second (or third) coat.

A good way to make sure that you have the right amount of paint on your brush is to pour some paint into a separate bucket or can, and dip your brush into this container. Dipping your brush into a full can of paint and then wiping off the excess against the edge causes a huge runny mess and leaves way too much paint on the brush.

1
(bleach)

2

3

If you've tried using the paint can as your trim bucket and you're not happy with the results — because the wire handle of the can is awkward to hold or because there is more pigment at the bottom of the can, causing your color to vary slightly — there is an alternative that can help.

You can create your own Ty-designed paint bucket with an easy-to-hold thumb handle. This awesome little creation allows you to hold the paint bucket and the ladder with one hand, leaving your other hand free to do the painting. All you need is an old plastic jug and a utility knife. Start to cut above the label and continue to carve away more than half off the top of the jug — be sure to leave the handle and the pour spout. Watch yourself with that knife!

Once you've finished cutting in the room with your favorite brush and your Ty-bucket, your new masterpiece mural might look a little unfinished. You're now ready to paint a classic masterpiece. But then again, abstract expressionism is also nice, so don't sweat it.

NOW YOU'RE ROLLING

Okay, Picasso, you're ready to roll. The trick to painting with a roller, as with a brush, is to have the right amount of paint loaded. Use a deep rolling tray to allow your roller to immerse itself in paint. Then, roll it a few times on the ridges of the tray to guard against drips.

When rolling paint on walls, it's best to do a section at a time. With each freshly dipped roller, paint up, then down until you've consistently covered an area about the width of two rollers. Be careful not to hit the ceiling or baseboard molding. Take your time. If time is not on your side, there is a quick way to avoid the little spots, called holidays, that don't get completely covered. The second coat usually covers holidays, but if you're painting with good quality paint, you may not need a second coat. As long as your paint has plenty of pigment, you might be able to paint a room in one coat. After checking the quality of the first wall, start slapping paint on the second wall while the first starts to dry. After you have coated the second wall heavily, go back to the first wall. This time, use a dry roller and lightly go over the wall again, blending the thick wet coat into a nice medium coat. Then, follow the same procedure for each of the remaining walls.

CLEAN UP YOUR ACT

It's not the *favorite* job of the day, but at least cleaning up is the *last* job of the day. But before you clean those brushes and rollers, make sure you've removed the painter's tape and checked for spots that you might have missed.

So, hopefully you've pulled off the tape without pulling off hunks of drywall too, and you've checked to see if there are any painting touch-ups to be done. Now, all that is left to do is clean your brushes and rollers. Some people (I'm not naming names!) like to save money and wash out rollers. Others would rather save the planet from all that paint going down the drain by just throwing away the rollers.

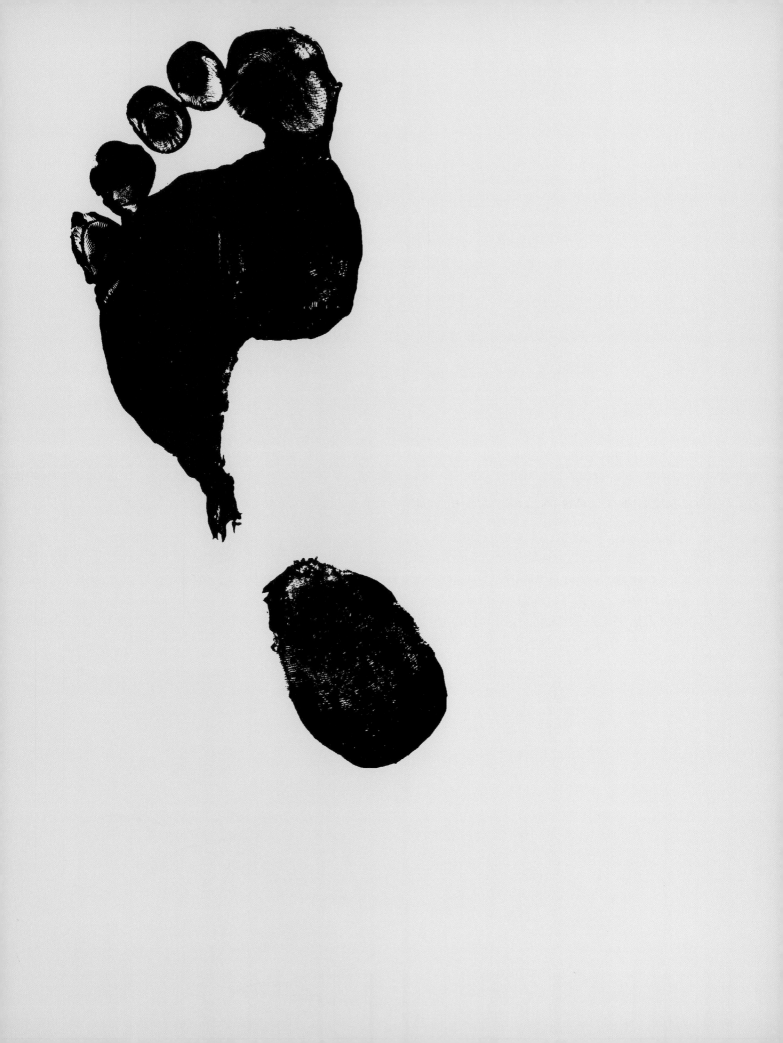

"Floors are like some people; they should be seen and not heard."

7
chapter

KEEPING YOUR TONGUE IN THE GROOVE

FLOORING

Floors get stepped on, dropped on, spilled on, and even have stuff dragged across their faces. It's hardly very surprising, then, that after a while some floors start to protest a little. My floors are so old that their squeaks sound like the angry squawks of a wronged bird. My CD player is totally drowned out by the squeaking and creaking of the floor as I cross the room to get the phone or the door. There is, of course, a logical reason: My house was built before plywood subflooring became a basic requirement in homes.

The builder of my original house simply nailed heart-of-pines flooring directly to the joists, which have settled along with the house, leaving enough dips and chips in the flooring for a Super Bowl party. But even if you have a subfloor, a lot depends on how well it was installed and how old it is. An addition (somewhat level) was built onto the back of my house in the '70s, but the subflooring was cheap and now squeals like a drunken mouse. I'm not sure which is worse.

Floors usually squeak because some of their boards have warped or buckled due to moisture damage, or because a joist below them has sagged. When you walk on them, the boards ride up and down, squeaking as they rub against the boards on each side of them. If you want to stop your floors from squeaking, there are a few simple tricks that will help you buy some time before that big floor renovation job eventually calls your name.

GETTING DOWN ON ALL FLOORS

TY'S STOP-THE-SQUEAK SOLUTIONS

Here are a few tricks to stop flooring boards from squeaking if you can access the floor from below.

A. To close gaps between a floor and its subfloor, predrill holes for several flathead wood screws about 1/4 inch shorter than the combined thickness of the finished floor and the subfloor. Since each is usually 3/4 inch thick, 1 1/4-inch screws should do. Ask a friend (or two) to stand on the floor to push it down flush with the subfloor or joist below, then screw through the subfloor and into the finished floor. This should close the gap. Be careful not to screw too tightly. If you have no friends, you can always use something heavy, such as a few concrete blocks.

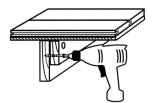

B. To close a small gap between the subfloor and the joist below it, use a piece of scrap 2-by-4 or 2-by-6 as a cleat. Place the cleat up flat against the joist and push it up against the bottom of the floor, then screw it to the side of the joist, pushing it up while you screw to eliminate the gap.

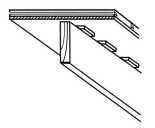

C. The quickest, easiest way to fix a squeak caused by a large gap between the subfloor and the joist below it is to insert a glue-coated shim.